Alfred Sandham

Coins, Tokens and Medals of the Dominion of Canada

Alfred Sandham

Coins, Tokens and Medals of the Dominion of Canada

ISBN/EAN: 9783337189709

Printed in Europe, USA, Canada, Australia, Japan

Cover: Foto ©Andreas Hilbeck / pixelio.de

More available books at **www.hansebooks.com**

COINS,

TOKENS AND MEDALS

OF THE

DOMINION OF CANADA;

BY

ALFRED SANDHAM,

LIFE MEMBER OF THE NUMISMATIC AND ANTIQUARIAN SOCIETY OF MONTREAL,
CORRESPONDING MEMBER AMER. NUM. & ARCH. SOCIETY OF NEW YORK.

ILLUSTRATED WITH 150 FAC-SIMILES OF COINS, MEDALS, &c.

MONTREAL:

DANIEL ROSE, PRINTER TO THE N. & A. S., 431 NOTRE DAME STREET.

1869.

Canadian Numismatic Publishing Institute — 1962

Reprinted by Canadian Numismatic Publishing Institute — Division of Regency
Coin & Stamp Co. Ltd., Rupert Ave., Winnipeg.

DEDICATED

TO THE

OFFICERS AND MEMBERS

OF

THE NUMISMATIC & ANTIQUARIAN SOCIETY

OF MONTREAL,

BY

ALFRED SANDHAM.

LIST OF ILLUSTRATIONS.

———

CONTENTS.

———

ERRATA.

Page 3, bottom line, for " included in the work the Medals, &c.," read "included, &c., illustrations of all the Medals."

Page 7, seventh line, for "taken from a work published in England by Rev., &c.," read, "from an article by Rev. Mr. Christmas."

Page 19, No. 4, should be "Obv. same as 5, &c."

Page 21, No. 3, for "6 cents," read "5 cents."

Page 22, No. 11, for "Rev. same as No. 10," read "same as No. 9."

Page 34, Plate 6, Fig. 7, should be attached to No. 73, instead of No. 72.

Page 41, in remarks on Nos. 5 to 16, for "Connects the Island of Repentiguy with that of Montreal," read "to connect Repentiguy with the Island of Montreal."

Page 70, No. 42, "Rev. In circle above 'PRESENTED,'" omit word "above."

COINS, TOKENS, &C.,

OF THE

DOMINION OF CANADA.

IT is our design, so far as the compass of this work will allow, to trace the history of our currency up to the present time, and by careful perusal, our Patrons will see that we have endeavored as far as possible to give a correct and faithful description of every coin known to us. It is possible that there may be in existence some specimen of which we have not heard, and probably some collectors may imagine they have found an error, but we can assure them that our facilities have been of such a character (having had access to some cabinets which contain the finest specimens of our coins) that the omissions cannot be either many or important. Should any of those who may receive this work notice an omission, we shall be happy to correspond with them upon the subject, and shall always be pleased to give, or receive any information which may tend to render the study of our coinage mutually agreeable and profitable. The compilation of this work has cost much time, thought, and correspondence, and to those kind friends in Canada and the United States who have aided us, we return our sincere thanks. In aiding us, they have conferred a favor upon every true Numismatist, for while there are exhaustive and able writers upon the Coinage of England; with Dickinson, Bushnell, Prime, and others upon the varied and interesting coins of the United States, yet the work now published is, we believe, the first upon the coins of Canada.

It was originally our intention to have included in this work, the

Medals of Canada, but to do them justice, (for some of them are of the very finest description), would have rendered it necessary to place the work at a much higher price, and thus frustrate our desire to place it within the reach of every collector.

Before proceeding further, we would say that this work is not issued as a mere matter of speculation, but from an ardent love for the Science of Numismatics, and a desire to render our Brethren that aid in their studies which we ourselves would have desired when passing through our initiation into the mysteries of the science. Should this object be attained we shall be satisfied.

The Currency, and particularly the Copper Currency of that portion of British North America, now known as the Dominion of Canada, consists chiefly of Tokens, many of which were issued by Banks or private individuals, while some were designed and struck in England, as a matter of speculation, and were sold in bulk to the merchants during the seasons of scarcity of change. Others, again, are the work of native artists. The number of the latter, however, is very small.

With reference to the money used in Canada prior to the Conquest in 1760, we have the following accounts taken from the Journal of the Travels of Professor Kalm of the University of Abo, in Sweden, in 1749; also from "Travels through Canada in 1805, by George Heriot, Esq., Dep. Postmaster General of British North America."

The following is Professor Kalm's account :

"The coins in use in Canada are the SOL, the LIVRE or FRANC, and CROWN or ECU. The SOL is the lowest, and is about the value of a penny in the English Colonies. The LIVRE or FRANC, contains 20 SOLS, and 3 LIVRES makes an ECU or CROWN. The SOLS consist of brass, with a very small mixture of silver, and those which I saw were worn thin by circulation. The supply of Coins however is limited, the greater part of the business of the colony being transacted with paper currency." Of this paper or card money we have a full description in the account given by Heriot, which is as follows:

" About the year 1700, the Trade of Canada was in a very languishing condition, which was to a great extent caused by the frequent alterations which took place in the medium of Exchange. The 'Company of the West Indies' (to whom the French Islands had been conceded) was permitted to circulate their small coin to the amount of 100,000 *francs*, but the use of this coin was prohibited in any other country. Owing to the want of specie in Canada, a decree was published, allowing this, and all other French coins to-be used, on augmentation of the value, one-fourth. At this period the *Intendant* of Canada experienced great trouble, not only in the payment of troops, but other expenses. On the 1st January, it was necessary to pay the officers and soldiers, and the funds remitted for that purpose, from France, generally arrived too late. To obviate this most urgent difficulty, the *Intendant*, with the sanction of the Council, issued notes, instead of money, always observing the increase in value of the coin. A *proces-verbal* was passed, and by virtue of an *ordinance* of the Governor General, and Intendant, there was stamped on each piece of this paper money (which was a card), its value, the signature of the Treasurer, an impression of the arms of France and (on sealing-wax) those of the Governor and Intendant. These were afterwards imprinted in France, with the same impressions as the current money of the Kingdom, and it was decreed that before the arrival in Canada, of the vessels from France, a particular mark should be added, to prevent the introduction of counterfeits.

" This species of money did not long remain in circulation and new cards were issued, on which new impressions were *engraved*, those under the value of four *livres* were distinguished by a particular mark made by the *Intendant*, while he signed those of four *livres* upward to six *livres*, and all above that amount, had, in addition, the signature of the Governor General. In the beginning of Autumn all these cards were brought to the Treasurer, who gave their value in Bills of Exchange on the Treasurer General of the Marine, or his deputy at Rochefort. Such cards as were worn, or spoiled, were not used again, but were burnt agreeably to an Act for that purpose.

" While these Bills of Exchange, were faithfully paid, the cards were preferred to specie, but when that punctuality was discontinued, they were no longer presented to the Treasurer, and the *Intendant*, (M. de Champigny) had much fruitless labor in trying to recall those which he had issued, and his successors were obliged to issue new cards every year, until they became so multiplied that their value was annihilated, and nobody would receive them.

" In 1713, the inhabitants offered to lose one-half, if the government would pay the other in specie. This offer was accepted, but was not carried into effect until 1717. But undeterred, by past experience, the Colony again commenced the issue of paper, (or card) money, and, in 1754 the amount was so large, that the Government was ' compelled to suspend to some future time the payment of it;' and in 1759, payment of Bills of Exchange given for this money was wholly suspended. When the colony passed into the hands of Britain, the Government paid to the Canadians an indemnity of £112,000 in bonds, and £24,000 sterling in specie, which was at the rate of 55 per cent. upon Bills of Exchange, and 34 per cent. on account of their paper money."

As we might reasonably expect, this card money soon disappeared entirely. Those redeemed in accordance with the terms named by Heriot were at once destroyed, and at the present day specimens of this, the first Canadian money are exceedingly rare, and whenever offered command exorbitant prices.

For the information of our readers we give the following fac-simile of one of these cards issued in 1729, and which bears the autograph of Governor Beauharnois, Intendant Hocquart and Comptroller Varin.

We have no account of the early currency of Canada beyond that quoted until 1790, when the Copper Company of Upper Canada issued a coin of which a full description is given in this work. This coin was struck in England for the Company, and cannot have been very extensively circulated, from the fact, that as far as we are aware no cabinet in Canada possesses a specimen. The description given in this book is taken from a work published in England by Rev. Mr. Christmas.

In the sale of the Mickly collection, at New York, in October, 1867, a coin was sold as a Kentucky piece, which had the obverse of this coin, Copper Company, &c., and for the reverse Hope presenting two children to Liberty, who stands surrounded by emblems of peace and plenty, with inscription, " British Settlement of Kentucky," This piece, (a proof,) sold for $40. It is from this coin we make the drawing found on Plate I.

The first coin or token of CANADIAN HOME MANUFACTURE, is the very coarsely executed but scarce and interesting politico-satirical token, commonly known as the Vexator Canadensis, issued in 1811.

The Native Artist who labored in the production of this token, evidently had not been a student for any length of time in a school of design, but still it appears that he was pleased with his own work, for several different specimens of this spoiled piece of copper are found in circulation.

The next issues were the various trade tokens of Nova Scotia, issued in 1814. Nova Scotia was the first colony which issued a regular coinage. In 1823 appeared the penny and half-penny tokens, bearing the bust of George IV on the obverse. Similar coins were issued in 1824 and 1832. It is somewhat remarkable to find coins of the latter date bearing the bust of George, as those who study history (which every numismatist must necessarily do,) are aware that William IV had then reigned two years. Passing over the intermediate years and their issues we arrive at 1837. It was in this year that the Canadian Rebellion burst forth, and one of its results was the introduction of a great proportion of those tokens, which now fill the Cabinets of Collectors.

It was about this time that the " Un Sou" series made their appearance, also many trade tokens, some of which, such as Molson, Brown, Mullins, &c., were struck to the order of the several firms, whose names they bear. The Banks of Montreal also issued a large number at the same time.

In 1838 and 1839, the Bank of Montreal issued a penny and half-penny token, known as the side view penny, &c., from the fact of its having for its obverse a front and side elevation of the building then occupied by them, and now known as the "Banque du Peuple," (People's Bank). These coins are now rare, particularly those of 1838, but few specimens of which are known, and these command very high prices.

In 1840, the first Prince Edward Island token makes its appearance, specimens of which are extremely rare. (See Plate IV, Fig. 2.) There are but four or five tokens from this Island, the one named and the 1855 and 1857 coins.

In 1843, New Brunswick launched her Frigate coins, which are very fine, and when in uncirculated condition, vie with any of the other provincial issues.

In 1856, Nova Scotia parted with the insignia of the land from whence she took her name, and in place of the Thistle donned the May-flower. These coins however were doomed to a short existance.

As early as the year 1822 a movement was made toward the introduction of a regular colonial decimal coinage, but no definite action was taken, until the year 1858, when the Canadian coinage, consisting of 20, 10 and 5 cent silver, and 1 cent copper coins made their appearance. These coins were issued through the Banks in the provinces, but the supply was not equal to the demand, consequently the old coppers and tokens, and the American and English silver still continue to form the greater bulk of the medium of exchange. Several ineffectual efforts have been made, to lessen the quantity of foreign silver in the Dominion, but with no other coinage to replace it, the supply has soon reached its former amount. It is earnestly to be desired that some steps should be taken, whereby we may have a Dominion Currency, and we have no doubt, but that a few years at most, will find the Wellingtons, Sous, Half-pennies and similar tokens, replaced by a coinage of which the New Dominion shall have no reason to feel ashamed. To return to our subject, Canada was not long permitted to stand alone in her experiment, for in the year 1861, New Brunswick introduced her really fine coinage, of the same denominations as Canada, but adding to the list the half cent. As if moved by the same spirit, Nova Scotia makes her appearance almost simultaneous with her sister province, and issues the cent and half cent, but does not issue any silver coins. This supply was supplemented by the issues of 1862 and 1864. Determined not to be outstript by these Colonies, old " *Prima Vista*," (Newfoundland,) in 1865, appears in the field, and without condescending to notice such *small* coin as half cents, strikes in nobler metal and issues a $2 Gold coin. To this was added a 20, 10 and 5 cent silver, and 1 cent copper, all of very neat design.

We have thus briefly sketched the history of the coinage, but before closing we may be permitted to add a few facts, which may not be uninteresting to our reader.

During the Rebellion of 1837 and 1838, several Merchants and others issued paper currency, commonly known as shin plasters, and among the most active in the work, was a merchant at Laprairie, (a village about nine miles above Montreal,) who established a bank called Henry's Bank, from which a very large number of notes were issued, of course with a *small* profit to the banker. At the close of the Rebellion the farmers in the vicinity held quite a large amount of this trash and were heavy losers, and even at the present day some specimens remain in their possession. They are, however, rarely offered for sale, and when in good condition are prized by Canadian collectors. Similar notes were issued by Messrs. Cuvillier & Sons, of Montreal. These, however, unlike the Henry issue, were redeemed by the firm who issued them, and are now extremely rare. There was a large variety issued by other parties, some of them being curiosities in their way, from the fact that the value is marked on the face of them, in almost every conceivable style. One in our possession is marked as good for—60 sous—half a dollar—two shillings and six pence—30 pence—trois francs—un ecu—the whole having in the centre a cut of the American half dollar of 1825, so that the most fastidious person must certainly be satisfied.

There are in circulation in Canada, a number of coins known as the Wellington series. These appear in many varieties, but we are of the opinion, that they were struck in England for export to any of the colonies where a scarcity of currency existed, the great bulk however finding its way to this colony. Wellington being a popular and familiar person, his bust was chosen as the most likely to meet the wishes of all parties. From the general circulation of these and other coins, they are sometimes classed as Canadian, therefore for the guidance of those who pursue this questionable mode of arranging their cabinets, we have given a description of some of the specimens, as well as of other coins, which we consider doubtful.

Before proceeding with the description of the various coins, we would say, that we place the Provinces in the order in which they stand in the history of our country, commencing with NEWFOUND-LAND which was discovered in 1499.

ABREVIATIONS.

G.—Gold.

B.—Bronze.

Obv.—Obverse.

Ins.—Inscription.

S.—Silver.

G. S.—German Silver.

Rev.—Reverse.

C.—Copper.

PLATE I.

NEWFOUNDLAND.

1. G. Obv. Head of Victoria, to left, laureated. " VICTORIA : D : G : REG : NEWFOUNDLAND." Rev. Within a beaded circle in three lines " 2 | DOLLARS | 1865 ; " outside circle, above, " TWO HUNDRED CENTS ;" below, " ONE HUNDRED PENCE." Milled edge. Plate 3, Fig. 5.

2. S. Obv. Bust of Victoria to left laureated. " VICTORIA D : G : REG : NEWFOUNDLAND." Rev. " 20 CENTS 1865 " within an ornamented and beaded circle. Milled edge.

3. S. Obv. Same as No. 2. Rev. do., do., " 10 CENTS 1865."

4. S. Obv. Same as No. 2. Rev. do., do., " 5 CENTS 1865."

5. C. Obv. Bust of Victoria to left laureated and draped. " VICTORIA D : G : REG : " Rev. Crowned date 1865 within a beaded circle, the whole surrounded with a wreath of oak, &c. " ONE CENT NEWFOUNDLAND." Plain edge. Plate 2, Fig. 6.

6. C. Obv. Arms of Rutherford. Rev. A fleece suspended. " R & I. S. RUTHERFORD. ST. JOHN'S NEWFOUNDLAND." Plate 2, Fig. 2.

7. C. Obv. Same as 6, date 1841 below. Rev. Same as 6.

8. C. Obv. Same as 6, date 1846 Rev. A fleece as in 6. " RUTHERFORD BROS HARBOUR GRACE NEWFOUNDLAND." The letter " H " in Harbour Grace comes immediately below the horn on fleece. In ribbon on top the first curves come immediately below letters " R R," and left end of ribbon under letter " E " in Rutherford. The right end extends towards " B " in Bros. Plate 2, Fig. 1.

9. C. Obv. Same as 8.   Rev. Same inscription, &c., but letters a little larger.   " H " in Harbour Grace comes on line with the horn. The ribbon extends further to right and left, and is at a greater distance from inscription.

10. C. Obv. Same as 8.   No date.   Rev. do.

11. C. Obv. " RESPONSIBLE GOVERNMENT AND FREE TRADE." Rev. Within a circle " 1860."   Outside of circle " FISHERY RIGHTS FOR NEWFOUNDLAND."   Edge plain.   Plate 2, Fig. 3.

NOVA SCOTIA.

1. C. Obv. Bust of Victoria to left, laureated and draped. " VIC-TORIA D : G : BRITT : REG : F : D : " Rev. Crowned date 1861 within a beaded circle, the whole surrounded by a heavy wreath composed of the Rose and May-flower. " ONE CENT NOVA SCOTIA." Plain edge. Plate 2, Fig. 8.

2. C. Obv. Same as No. 1. Rev. do., do., " HALF CENT."

There are issues of Nos. 1 and 2 bearing date 1862 and 1864, all plain edge.

3. C. Obv. Small bust of George III., to right, laureated and draped. " HALF PENNY TOKEN 1815." Rev. Ship in full sail to right. " PAYABLE BY JOHN ALEXR. BARRY. HALIFAX." Plain edge. Plate 4, Fig. 4.

4. C. Obv. Large bust of George III., otherwise same as No. 3. Rev. Same as No. 3.

5. C. Small bust of George III., to right, laureated and draped, within a circle, " HALF PENNY TOKEN. 1814." Rev. Front eleva-tion of Government House. " PAYABLE BY HOSTERMAN & ETTER HALIFAX." Plain edge. Plate 3, Fig. 7.

6. C. Large bust of George III., without the circle, date " 1815," otherwise same as No. 5. Rev. Same as No. 5. Although bearing a larger bust this coin is much smaller than No. 5.

7. C. Obv. A large bust of George III., to right, laureated and draped. " HALF PENNY TOKEN 1814." Rev. A frigate under sail,

to right, " PAYABLE BY CARRITT & ALPORT HALIFAX." Edge milled. Plate 3, Fig. 1.

8. C. Obv. Military bust, to left, " BROKE HALIFAX NOVA, SCOTIA." Rev. Britannia seated. In the distance to left two ships " BRITANNIA 1814." Edge milled. Plate 3, Fig. 6.

9. C. Obv. Indian with bow and arrow. A dog by his side. " STARR & SHANNON HALIFAX. 1815." Rev. Ship under sail, to right, "HALF PENNY TOKEN NOVA SCOTIA." Edge plain. Plate 2, Fig. 7.

10. C. Obv. Indian as on No. 9. " COMMERCIAL CHANGE." Rev. Same as No. 9.

11. C. Obv. A cask marked "Nails and Spikes," between a Scythe-blade and a Sickle; above it two spades crossed. " PAYABLE AT W. A. & S. BLACK'S HALIFAX N. S." Rev. Front view of a house. " WHOLESALE & RETAIL HARDWARE STORE 1816." Edge plain.

12. C. Obv. Same as No. 11. " HALIFAX NOVA SCOTIA." Rev. Same as No. 11. Plate 3, Fig. 3.

13. C. Obv. Within a circle, a cask marked "Spikes, Nails &c. "HALF PENNY TOKEN 1815." Rev. " IMPORTERS OF IRON MON-GERY HARDWARE &C." Within a circle in six lines, " PAYABLE | BY | MILES W. | WHITE | HALIFAX | N. S." Plate 3, Fig. 2.

14. C. Obv. Bust of George III. to right, laureated and draped. "HALF PENNY TOKEN 1815." Rev. Ship in full sail to right, in the distance to the left, another vessel. " HALIFAX." Edge milled. The bust on this coin, is the same type as the English half-penny of 1806.

15. C. Obv. Bust of George IV. to the left, laureated and draped.

PLATE II.

"PROVINCE OF NOVA SCOTIA." Rev. A two leaved thistle. "ONE PENNY TOKEN 1823." Engrailed edge.

16. C. Obv. Same as No. 15. Rev. do., do., "HALF-PENNY TOKEN 1823." There are specimens of Nos. 15 & 16 bearing dates of 1824 and 1832.

17. C. Obv. Bust of Victoria to right, filletted and the neck bare. "PROVINCE OF NOVA SCOTIA." Rev. Two leaved thistle. "ONE PENNY TOKEN 1840." Engrailed edge. Plate 1, Fig. 3.

18. C. Obv. Same as No. 17. Rev. do., do., "HALF-PENNY TOKEN."

These coins (17 & 18) are very inferior in point of workmanship, to those bearing the head of George IV. The penny and half-penny of this type, occur with the dates 1840, 1843 and 1856. Very fine specimens of Nos. 15 to 18 are sometimes met with, but no proofs are known to exist.

19. C. Obv. Head of Victoria, to the left, wearing open Coronet, of which only the front is seen, the neck bare. "VICTORIA D: G: BRITANNIAR: REG: F: D: 1856." Rev. A large sprig of May-flower. "PROVINCE OF NOVA SCOTIA   ONE PENNY TOKEN." Plain edge. Plate 1, Fig. 2.

20. C. Obv. Same as No. 19. Rev. do., do., "HALF-PENNY."

21. C. Obv. Ship in full sail to right. "NOVA SCOTIA AND NEW BRUNSWICK SUCCESS." Rev. Female seated on a bale of Goods, holding in her right hand a pair of Scales, in her left a Cornucopia. A vessel in the distance. "HALF-PENNY TOKEN." Milled edge. Rare. Plate 3, Fig. 4.

22. C. Obv. Ship in full sail. " PAYABLE AT THE STORE OF J. BROWN." Rev. Four leaved thistle. " NEMO ME IMPUNE LA-CESSIT."

23. C. Obv. " ROBERT PURVES, CHEAP FAMILY STORE, WAL-LACE." Rev, " ENCOURAGE COUNTRY IMPORTERS." Plate 4, Fig. 3.

MAGDALEN ISLAND.

1. C. Obv. Within a circle, a Seal. " MAGDALEN ISLAND TOKEN 1815." Rev. Within a circle, a Codfish. " SUCCESS TO THE FISHERY, ONE PENNY." Edge engrailed. Plate 4, Fig. 5.

PRINCE EDWARD ISLAND.

1. C. Obv. Sheaf of Wheat with sickle. "PRINCE EDWARD ISLAND HALF-PENNY 1840." Rev. A plough. "COMMERCE AND TRADE." Very rare. Edge plain. Plate 4, Fig. 2.

2. C. Obv. A Plough. "SPEED THE PLOUGH." Rev. A Codfish. "SUCCESS TO THE FISHERIES." Several varieties of this coin (which was struck in 1840), are in circulation. The difference being in the shape of the plough. Plate 4, Fig. 6.

3. C. Obv. "PRINCE EDWARD'S ISLAND 1855." Rev. "SELF GOVERNMENT AND FREE TRADE." Edge plain. Plate 4, Fig. 7.

4. C. Obv. Same as No. 3, "1857." Rev. do., do.

5. C. Obv. "PRINCE EDWARD ISLAND 1855." Rev. Same as No. 3.

6. C. Obv. Steamship to left. "HALF PENNY TOKEN." Rev. "FISHERIES AND AGRICULTURE." Plate 4, Fig. 1.

NEW BRUNSWICK.

1. C. Obv. Bust of Victoria to left, wearing an open crown. VICTORIA DEI GRATIA REGINA. 1843." Rev. A frigate with full rigging, but without sails. "NEW BRUNSWICK, ONE PENNY TOKEN."

2. C. Obv. Same as No. 1. Rev. do., do. "HALF-PENNY."

Bronze proofs of these coins are often met with, and are of the highest order of workmanship.

3. C. Obv. Bust of Victoria to the left, filleted. " VICTORIA DEI GRATIA REGINA 1854." Rev. Frigate as on No. 1. NEW BRUNS-WICK, ONE PENNY CURRENCY."

4. C. Obv. Same as No. 3. Rev. do., do., " HALF-PENNY." Plate 2, Fig. 5.

5. C. Obv. Bust of Victoria to left, draped and laureated. " VIC-TORIA D: G: BRITT: REG: F: D:" Rev. Crowned date 1861 within a wreath, " ONE CENT, NEW BRUNSWICK."

6. C. Obv. Same as No. 5. Rev. do., do., " HALF CENT."

There is also a variety of 5 and 6 bearing date " 1864."

7. C. Obv. Ship in full sail to right. " FOR PUBLIC ACCOMMO-DATION." Rev. " ST. JOHN NEW BRUNSWICK HALF-PENNY TOKEN." Edge milled. Plate 2, Fig. 4.

8. B. Obv. Arms. " DEPOSITORY OF ARTS." Rev. " F. M'DER-MOTT, IMPORTER OF ENGLISH, FRENCH & GERMAN FANCY GOODS KING ST., SNT. JOHN, N. B." Very rare. Plate 3, Fig. 8.

PLATE III.

CANADA.

1. S. Obv. Head of Victoria to left, laureate. "VICTORIA DEI GRATIA REGINA, CANADA." Rev. Within two Maple branches, "20 CENTS 1858," in three lines, surmounted by a crown. Milled edge. Plate 4, Fig. 8.

2. S. Obv. Same as No. 1. Rev. do., do. "10 CENTS." Milled edge.

3. S. Obv. Same as No. 1. Rev. do., do. "6 CENTS." Milled edge.

There are also specimens of these coins with plain edge, which are very rare.

4. C. Obv. A River god, with trident in left hand, leans his right hand on an urn from which water flows. On the exergual line "PONTHON;" in exergue "1794." Legend, on a raised border. "FERTILITATEM DIVITASQUE CIRCUMFEREMUS." Rev. "COPPER COMPANY OF UPPER CANADA ONE HALF PENNY." Plate 1, Fig. 9, shows reverse of this coin.

5. C. Obv. Coarsely executed head to right, "VEXATOR CANADIN SIS." Rev. Rude figure of woman dancing, "RENUNTER VISCAPE 1811." Plate 6, Fig. 1.

6. C. Obv. same as No. 5. "VEXATOR CANADIENSIS." Rev. Same as No. 5.

7. C. Obv. Same as No. 5. "VEXATOR CANADENSIS 1811." Rev. Same as No. 5. "RENUNILLUS VISCAPE."

There are two other varieties of this coin, the difference consisting in the mode of spelling, or in punctuation.

8. C. Obv. Sloop under sail to right. "HALF PENNY TOKEN UPPER CANADA." Rev. An Indian as in No. 9 of Nova Scotia coins. In exergue "1815." "COMMERCIAL CHANGE."

9. C. Obv. Ship under sail to right. "SUCCESS TO THE COM-MERCE OF UPP^R AND LOW^R CANADA." Rev. "SUCCESS TO COM-MERCE, AND PEACE TO THE WORLD 1816." Plate 6, Fig. 2.

10. C. Obv. Same as No. 9. Rev. "SIR ISAAC BROCK, BART., THE HERO OF UPPER CANADA WHO FELL AT THE GLORIOUS BAT-TLE OF QUEENSTOWN HEIGHTS ON THE 13TH OCT^R 1812." Milled edge.

11. C. Obv. Two Angels holding a wreath over an urn placed on a pedestal, inscribed, "FELL OCT. 13, 1812." "SIR ISAAC BROCK, THE HERO OF UP^R CANADA." Rev. Same as No. 10.

The design on the obverse of this coin was taken from the original monument, erected in memory of Sir Isaac Brock, on the Queenstown Heights. It was maliciously blown up by a person named Lett, who was afterwards imprisoned for robbery in the United States. It has been replaced by a handsome monument, by the loyal subjects of Her Majesty in Upper Canada, (now Ontario.)

12. C. Obv. Bust of Duke of Wellington to left, laureated. Within a circle, "HALF PENNY TOKEN 1816." Rev. Ship under sail to right. Within circle, "MONTREAL." Plate 7, Fig. 8.

13. C. Obv. Bust of George IV. to right, laureated and draped. "TOKEN 1820." Rev. A beaver. "NORTH WEST COMPANY." Engrailed edge. This coin is exceedingly rare, no specimen known to be in Canada.

14. C. Obv. Same as No. 8. Bowsprit of Sloop extends over the last letter in the word Canada. Rev. An anvil; above it, two spades crossed, below 1820. Edge milled.

15. C. Obv. Same as No. 8. Bowsprit of Sloop extends between letters "D" and "A" in Canada. Rev. Same as No. 14.

16. C. Obv. Same as No. 15. Rev. A cask, inscribed, "UPPER CANADA ;" below, "1821 COMMERCIAL CHANGE."

17. C. Obv. Justice standing with sword and scales. " LESSLIE & SONS, TORONTO AND DUNDASS 1822." Rev. A plough, above it, "TOKEN;" below it, " 2D CURRENCY." " PROSPERITY TO CANADA, LA PRUDENCE ET LA CANDEUR " Rare. Plate 5, Fig. 7.

18. C. Obv. Same as No. 17. " LESSLIE & SONS, YORK KINGS-TON & DUNDAS." Rev. A plough with one bar across handles, above it, " TOKEN." below, "HALF PENNY." Same inscription as No. 17.

There are several varieties of this half-penny token, the difference consisting in the shape of the plough, and some having two bars across the handles. No corresponding penny has yet been met with,

19. C. Obv. Same as No. 14. Rev. A plough, "TO FACILITATE TRADE 1823." Edge milled.

20. C. Obv. Same as No. 15. Rev. Same as 19.

21. C. Obv. " CANADA 1830." Rev. "HALF PENNY," in two lines. Plate 5, Fig. 6.

22. C. Obv. Bust of George IV to the left, laureated and draped. " PROVINCE OF UPPER CANADA." Rev. Britannia as on English coinage of 1806. " HALF PENNY TOKEN 1832." Edge engrailed. Plate 6, Fig. 3.

23. C. Obv. Same as No. 14. Rev. Same as No. 19, dated " 1833."

24. C. Obv. Same as No. 15. Rev. Same as No. 23.

5. Brass. Obv. Same as No. 8, Bowsprit of Sloop almost touching the apex of last letter in " Canada." Rev. An anvil, with hammer

and tongs, between a scythe-blade and a vice; above it, two spades crossed; below, " 1833."

26. C. Obv. A *habitant* or French Canadian Farmer, standing with a whip in his right hand and the left extended. "PROVINCE DU BAS CANADA DEUX SOUS." Rev. Arms of City of Montreal. "BANK TOKEN ONE PENNY 1837." In the scroll proceeding from both sides of the garter in Arms, in sunk letters, "BANK OF MONTREAL." Plate 1, Fig. 4.

27. C. Obv. Same as No. 26. Rev. do., do. In scroll, "CITY BANK."

28. C. Obv. Same as No. 26. Rev. do., do. In scroll, "BANQUE DU PEUPLE."

29. C. Obv. Same as No. 26. Rev. do., do. "QUEBEC BANK."

30. C. Obv. Front view of Bank of Montreal, now occupied by Banque du Peuple. "PROVINCE OF CANADA BANK OF MONTREAL." Rev. Same as No. 27. Plate 1, Fig. 5, shows obverse of coin.

This coin is rare. The specimen from which the drawing is made, is the only one we have met with, all the other coins bearing the same view of building, being dated 1842.

31. C. Obv. Same as 26, " UN SOU." Rev. do., do. "HALF PENNY."

There are also the three other varieties of this half-penny, corresponding with Nos. 27, 28 & 29.

32. C. Obv. "FRANCIS MULLINS & SON IMPORTERS OF SHIP CHANDLERY &C MONTREAL." Rev. Ship in full sail to right. "COMMERCE TOKEN." Milled edge. Plate 5, Fig. 3.

33. C. Obv. Two Maple leaves crossed. "COMMERCE BAS CANADA." Rev. Within a wreath, " UN SOU J. ROY MONTREAL." Scarce in good condition. Plate 5, Fig. 4.

34. C. Obv. Within a circle, a cask; above, "BREWERS," below, "DISTILLERS &C., &C., &C." On either sides, "UN SOU." Without the circle, "THS & WM MOLSON MONTREAL." Rev. Within a circle, Distillery Apparatus, &c. "CASH PAID FOR ALL SORTS OF GRAIN 1837." Milled edge. Scarce. Plate 7, Fig. 6.

35. C. Obv. Same as 25, without date. Rev. "T. S. BROWN & CO IMPORTERS OF HARDWARES MONTREAL." Plate 5, Fig. 1.

The following extracts from a letter, received from Mr. Brown, give the history of this token, and at the same time, serve as an explanation for the appearance of many of our other tokens.

"Being in Birmingham in the year 1832, I learned that many of the Copper Coins circulating in Canada had in time past, when there was no prohibition, been issued by traders in England. Thinking they would be a good means of advertising for myself, and the trade being free with us, I told a house from whom I was purchasing, to put up a lot, and they shipped two casks weighing about 400 or 500 lbs. each. These all bore the stamp "T. S. BROWN & CO. IMPORTERS OF HARDWARES MONTREAL," with emblems of the trade. These made sixty to the pound; and cost, including the expense of dies, one shilling and five pence sterling per pound. Nominally each pound represented two shillings and six pence currency, at which price I sold them out rapidly, for there happened to be at the moment a scarcity, and there was a constant run for them by people buying five to ten dollars worth at a time. The cholera of that year suspended trade, and I wished I had imported nothing but "Coppers." But I never repeated the experiment, for they soon after came from all quarters and became a "drug." Those I sold—the amount was about four or five hundred dollars—continued a portion of our "currency," and now, at the end of thirty-five years, a stray one is sometimes found in circulation."

36. C. Obv. A Tea-kettle between a vice and hand-saw; above, a

Scythe blade and Spade crossed; below, a knife and fork crossed. Rev. " J. SHAW & CO IMPORTERS OF HARDWARES UPPER TOWN QUEBEC." Milled edge. Plate 5, Fig. 2.

In a letter from Mr. Shaw, he says, " This coin was imported from Birmingham, in 1837, and was issued the same year, but I do not know the name of the Die-Sinker, nor the quantity imported."

37. C. Obv. Ship in full sail to right. " FOR. PUBLIC ACCOM-MODATION." Rev. " CANADA HALF PENNY TOKEN," in four lines.

The following coins compose what is familiarly known among Canadian collectors as the " Un Sou series." It will be noticed that from the description given of them, that many are somewhat similar in appearance, the difference consisting merely in the arrangement of the flowers which compose the boquet, or in the number of leaves on the reverse. Figures 5, 6 and 7, on Plate 6, will illustrate the mode of description chosen by us.

38. C. Obv. Boquet consisting of Roses, Thistle, Shamrock and Wheat. 1 Rose and bud, 3 shamrocks, 5 rose leaves and 1 head wheat to right; 2 thistles, 2 thistle leaves, 1 head wheat and 2 shamrocks to left. Large thistle leaf in centre of boquet; the head of wheat on right bends immediately over the rose ; the whole bound with ribbon having bow to right and two ends to left. " AGRICUL-TURE AND COMMERCE * BAS-CANADA*" Rev. Wreath with nine leaves to right and eight to left ; between each leaf a small sprig with berry similar to holly. " UN SOU " within wreath. " TOKEN MON-TREAL." Edge plain.

39. C. Obv. Boquet as No. 38. 1 Rose, 4 leaves, 3 shamrocks and 1 head of wheat to right; 2 thistles, 3 shamrocks, 1 head wheat and 4 leaves (probably intended for Maple leaves) to left, bound with ribbon, bow to left, ribbons to right. Inscription same as No. 38. Rev. Wreath of 16 leaves, 8 on either side. Bow connecting them forms a triangle,

PLATE IV

heavy at top but smaller towards wreath. Same inscription as No, 38. Over letter " o " in Sou is a small dot. Edge plain.

40. C. Obv. Boquet. 1 Rose, 4 leaves, 3 shamrocks, 1 blade of wheat to right ; 2 thistle heads with blades of wheat between, 2 this-tle leaves, 1 shamrock, 1 head and 2 blades wheat to left; a thistle leaf in centre, reaching two-thirds up boquet; on top a head of wheat slightly inclined to right. Same inscription as No. 38. Rev. Same as No. 39. Bow somewhat heavier and no dot over letter " o." Word " MONTREAL " almost touches bottom of wreath. Edge plain.

41. C. Obv. Boquet. 1 Rose, 5 rose leaves, 1 shamrock and 1 head of wheat to right; 2 thistle heads with shamrock between, 3 shamrocks, 1 rose leaf. 1 head and 1 blade wheat to left. In centre a rose leaf; on top 2 blades wheat parallel to each other and slightly inclined to right. Bow of ribbon to right, ends to left. Same in-scription as No. 38. Rev. Same as No. 39, but bow more flat, and on either side a sprig similar to those between the leaves. Ribbon entwined round stems of wreath. Same inscription, but more space between it and wreath. Milled edge.

42. C. Obv. Boquet. 1 Rose, 4 rose leaves, 2 shamrocks and 1 head of wheat to right; 2 thistles, 2 thistle leaves, 3 blades and 1 head wheat, and 1 shamrock to left; in centre, large thistle leaf; on top, blade of wheat slightly bent : stems of boquet very small. Bow small, to right ; long ribbon to left. Same inscription. Rev. Wreath as in No. 39. Bow very large triangle. Bottom of left wreath touches letter " R " in Montreal. Leaves in wreath much closer than in No. 39. Same inscription. Edge plain.

43. C. Obv. Boquet. 1 Rose, 7 rose leaves, 2 blades and 1 head wheat, to right ; 2 thistles, 2 shamrocks, 3 blades and 1 head wheat, with large leaf (as in No. 39,) to left, a similar leaf turns into centre of boquet; on top, 1 head and 1 broad blade of wheat, the former

inclined to left, the latter to right. Two blades of wheat to right and left almost touch letters " ʊ " and " т " in Agriculture, and "ᴍᴍ" in Commerce. Slender bow to right ; 2 long ribbons to left. Same inscription. Rev. Wreath of 18 leaves, equally divided with sprigs, &c., between each. Leaves at top of wreath almost meeting. Very small bow, with ribbon encircling ends of wreath, which nearly touch letters " ɴ " and " ᴇ " in Montreal. The words " ᴜɴ soᴜ " close together. Same inscription. Edge plain.

44. C. Obv. Same as No. 43, but cracked die crossing letter " o " in Commerce, over top of boquet, reaching two-thirds across the coin. Rev. Very open wreath of 17 leaves, 8 to right, 9 to left. No bow, but two of the leaves start from juncture of wreath, extending upwards like letter V, close to letters " s " and " ʊ " in sou. Letters in Un Sou close like No. 43, and small dot over " o." Ends of wreath much spread, extending from letters " ɴ " to " ᴇ " in Montreal. Same inscription. Edge plain.

45. C. Obv. Boquet. 1 Rose, 3 rose leaves, 2 shamrocks, 4 blades and 1 head wheat, to right ; 2 thistles, 2 shamrocks, 1 head and 2 blades of wheat, 4 leaves (as in No. 39) to left, one of these being between two thistles, the other turned over into centre ; on top 3 blades wheat, 1 straight, the others bent to right and left. Blade of wheat to left passes between letters " ʀ " and " ɪ " in Agriculture. Bow to right, ribbon to left, inclined downwards. Inscription same, but more space between words Bas Canada. Rev. Wreath of 18 leaves, with sprigs between, equally divided ; small and flat bow with sprig on either side ; top leaves of wreath almost touching. Word Montreal being very close to wreath. Same inscription. Edge plain.

46. C Obv. Same as 45, but slight difference in arrangement. Rev. Same as 45.

47. C. Obv. Very open boquet Rose, 4 rose leaves, 3 shamrocks, 1 blade wheat, to right; 2 thistles, 2 shamrocks, 2 blades and 1 head wheat, 3 leaves same as No. 39, to left; 1 leaf to centre ; on top, 1 blade wheat slightly bending to left; long open bow to right; 2 ribbons curved downwards to left. " AGRICULTURE & COMMERCE : BAS— CANADA." Rev. Same as No. 45, dot over " o " in Sou.

48. C. Obv. Boquet still more open than No. 47. 1 Rose, 4 leaves, 4 shamrocks, 1 head wheat, to right; 2 thistles,—1 straight upwards, —3 shamrocks, 1 blade wheat which touches top of upper thistle,— 1 head wheat immediately above it, 3 leaves as in No. 39, 1 turns over centre on top, 3 blades wheat, curved right and left ; large and open bow to left ; single short ribbon to right. " * AGRICULTURE & COM MERCE * BAS-CANADA." Letters poor, no cross line on letters " A." Rev. Same as No. 45, letters a little more open. Edge plain.

49. C. Obv. Boquet heavy, to left. 1 Rose, 5 rose leaves, one of which turns to centre, 4 broad blades wheat to right; 2 thistles, 2 thistle leaves, one turning to centre, 1 shamrock, 5 blades wheat, one between thistles, to left; on top a head wheat; the whole bound by ribbon, which extends about a quarter inch to right and left. " * AGRI- CULTURE & COMMERCE * BAS-CANADA." Rev. Very close wreath, same as No. 45, large bow curved to left with leaves close to it ; wreath somewhat orange shaped and leaves very large. " UN SOU " very much spread, and dot over " o ;" word " MONTREAL " close to wreath. Edge plain.

50. C. Obv. Same as No. 49. Rev. Same, bow curved to right.

51. C. Obv. Small boquet. 1 Rose, 4 rose leaves, 2 shamrocks, 2 broad blades and 1 head wheat, to right; 2 thistles, 2 broad blades and 1 head wheat, 3 leaves as No. 39, one in centre to left; on top, between heads of wheat a blade of same broken and bent down,

tops of boquet close to inscription, which is same as No. 49, small bow to right, ribbon to left. Rev. Same as No. 49, but without dot on " o." Edge plain.

52. C. Obv. Boquet. 1 Rose, 4 rose leaves, one turned to left, 1 shamrock, 1 blade wheat to right; 2 thistles, 1 shamrock, 4 blades wheat, and 2 leaves as No. 39, one over centre to left; on top, 3 heads wheat, two inclined to left, the other broken and bent downwards to right. Bow short and open to right; 2 ribbons to left. Inscription same as No. 49. Rev. Same as No. 49. Edge plain.

53. C. Obv. Very full boquet. 2 Thistles, 1 small and 2 large thistle leaves to right—one of the large leaves turns over and forms centre of boquet; 1 large rose, 5 rose leaves, one of which turns over centre thistle leaf. sprig of 3 shamrocks to left; on top 2 heads of wheat to right and left, and 3 blades wheat between. Bow to left, short ribbon hanging downwards, to right. " AGRICULTURE & COMMERCE BAS CANADA." Rev. Same as No. 49. Edge milled.

54. C. Obv. Very small boquet. 1 Rose, 4 leaves, 1 head and 1 blade wheat to right; 2 thistles, 1 blade wheat, 2 leaves as No. 39 to left—one turns over centre on top; 2 heads wheat with blade between each, inclined to left; bow and ribbon to right; ribbon to left. " : AGRICULTURE & COMMERCE : BAS-CANADA." Rev. Wreath of 18 leaves, very much spread, top leaves just touching; bow with long ribbon which entwines round ends of wreath; sprigs on each side of bow; bottom of wreath nearly touches word " MONTREAL ;" dot over " o " in Sou. Plain edge.

55. Brass. Obv. Very open boquet. 1 Rose, 5 leaves, 1 shamrock, 1 head wheat to right; 2 thistles, 4 shamrocks, one between thistles, 1 rose leaf which turns over centre; 1 head and 1 blade of wheat to left; on top, in centre, 2 blades wheat curved to right; large

open bow to left, long ribbon to right. " • AGRICULTURE & COM-
MERCE • BAS-CANADA." Rev. Small wreath of 16 leaves with sprigs.
Bow with sprigs on either side, and flowing ribbon entwined round
ends of wreath. No dot over "o" in Sou. Edge plain. Scarce.

56. C. Obv. Boquet as in No. 55, with 2 rose leaves instead of 1
to left. Bottom of boquet more open. Rev. Same as No. 55, but
ribbon which entwines end of wreath is much more slender.

57. C. Obv. Boquet. 1 Rose, 6 leaves, 2 blades and 1 head
wheat to right; 2 thistles, 2 shamrocks, 2 leaves as No. 39, (one
over centre,) 1 head and 1 blade wheat to left; in centre 1 head
wheat inclined to left. No bow, 2 flowing ribbons right and left.
Inscription same as No. 49. Rev. Open wreath of 18 leaves. Triangular bow inclined to right; ribbons lying parallel to ends of wreath;
wreath close to word "MONTREAL." Edge plain.

58. C. Obv. Full boquet. 1 Rose, 3 leaves, 3 shamrocks, 3 blades
and 1 head wheat, to right; 2 thistles, 2 shamrocks, 4 leaves (as in
No. 39), 1 head and 2 blades wheat to left; on top 3 blade swheat, 1
straight upwards, 1 inclined to right and touching letter "c" in Commerce; the other to left and touching bottom of "R" in Agriculture; one blade wheat passes between letters "R" and "I" in same
word; long open bow to right, 2 ribbons to left. ": AGRICULTURE
& COMMERCE : BAS-CANADA." Rev. Very open wreath of 18 leaves,
almost touching at top. No bow; 2 bottom leaves extending as in
No. 44; ends of wreath touch letters "N" and "R" in Montreal.
Dot over letter "o" in Sou. Edge plain.

59. C. Obv. Boquet. 1 Rose, 4 leaves, 4 shamrocks, 1 head
wheat to right; 2 thistles, 2 shamrocks, 2 blades and 1 head wheat,
4 leaves as No. 39, one over centre, to left, 2 blades wheat at top to
right and left; open bow to left; short ribbon to right. " • AGRI-
CULTURE & COMMERCE • BAS-CANADA." Rev. Same as 58.

60. C. Obv. Open boquet. 1 Rose, 6 rose leaves, 3 shamrocks, 1 head and 1 blade wheat, to right; 2 thistles, 3 thistle leaves, one forming centre, 2 blades and 1 head wheat, to left.; on top in centre 1 blade wheat; very long flowing ribbon to right and left. "* AGRI-CULTURE & COMMERCE * BAS-CANADA." Die cracked across letters " U " and " L " in Agriculture. Rev. Open wreath of 18 leaves, no bow, but leaves as in No. 44; sprigs and branches very light. Both ends of wreath pass close to last stroke of " N " in Montreal. " UN SOU " more extended, and no dot over " O." Edge plain.

61. C. Obv. Same as No. 53. Rev. Open wreath of 18 leaves. Slender triangular bow with two ribbons below, close to letters " T " and " E " in Montreal. Words " UN SOU " close together; dot over, and very close to letter " O." Edge plain.

62. C. Obv. Boquet. 1 Rose, 5 leaves, 2 shamrocks, 1 head wheat, to right; 2 thistles, 2 thistle leaves, one over centre, 1 leaf as in No. 39 between thistles, and 1 head wheat, to left; open bow to left; 2 ribbons to right. "* AGRICULTURE & COMMERCE * BAS-CANADA." Rev. Open wreath of 20 leaves, with sprigs; top leaf but one on right side almost touches letter " N " in Token. Flat open bow.

63. Brass. Same as No. 62.

64. C. Obv. 1 Rose, 6 leaves, 1 shamrock, 1 blade and 1 head wheat, to right; 2 thistles, 2 leaves, one over centre, 1 head and 4 blades of wheat, to left, one of which touches letter " L " in Agriculture; long ribbon to left and right. "* AGRICULTURE & COMMERCE * BAS-CANADA." Rev. Close wreath of 20 leaves. Very large open bow with ribbon entwined round stem of wreath, which nearly touches letters " N " and " E " in Montreal. Dot over " O " being near upper line.

65. C. Obv. Same as 62, but flowers little differently arranged. Rev. Same as 58.

66. C. Obv. Boquet. 1 Rose with bud, 3 leaves, 2 heads and 1 blade wheat to right; 1 thistle, 2 leaves, 2 shamrocks, 1 blade and 1 head wheat to left. No bow, strings to right and left. Same inscription as No. 64. Rev. Wreath of laurel, (32 leaves) with sprigs between. Very large open bow with ribbon over front of wreath. One end of ribbon on letter " T," the other between " R " and " E " in Montreal. Dot over " o " Edge plain.

67. C. Obv. Boquet. 1 Rose, 6 leaves, 2 heads and 3 blades wheat to right; very large thistle, 1 leaf, 3 shamrocks, 2 broad blades wheat, to left. Ribbon same as No. 66. Inscription punctuated same as No. 64, but words very close to each other. Rev. same as No. 66. Edge plain.

68. Brass. Same as No. 66.

69. C. Obv. Boquet, (very open). 1 Rose, 8 leaves, 2 of which (near the top of Boquet) turn over towards left, 1 shamrock and 1 head of wheat to right; large thistle, 2 leaves, 3 shamrocks, 1 head and 2 blades wheat, to left; on top, sprig of shamrock with 3 leaves. Very long ribbons to right and left. Top of boquet quite close to the inscription, which is the same as on No. 64. Rev. Wreath as on No. 66, but with 40 leaves, 22 to right and 18 to left; same bow as No. 66, but end of ribbon to left turns upwards immediately over letter " T." No dot over " o " in Sou. The words " UN SOU " are inclined towards right side of the wreath. Edge plain.

70. C. Obv. Boquet. 1 Rose and bud with 4 leaves, 4 shamrocks, 1 head of wheat, inclined over rose to right; 2 thistles, 3 leaves (one forming centre), 2 shamrocks, 1 rose leaf, 2 blades and 1 head wheat, to left; on top, 3 blades wheat. Very slender, open bow to right, 2 ribbons to left. Same inscription as No. 59. Rev. Wreath of 17 leaves, 9 to right, 8 to left; slender triangular bow and small ribbon. Stem of left side of wreath, passes between " R " and " E " in Montreal; top of wreath very open. Edge plain.

71. C. Obv. Boquet. 2 thistles, 3 leaves, (2 large and 1 small,) one of the large ones forming centre of boquet; 3 blades and 1 head of wheat, to right; 1 rose, 5 leaves, (one turning over centre thistle leaf,) 3 leaved sprig of shamrock, 5 blades and 1 head of wheat to left. Small, but thick bow to left, short ribbons hanging down to right. Head of wheat to right nearly touches first " M " in Commerce. "AGRICULTURE & COMMERCE BAS CANADA." Rev. Heavy wreath of 24 Maple leaves, connected by a double bow; ribbons entwined round ends of wreath, top leaves of which touch each other. In centre of wreath in very bold letters " UN SOU." Inscription, " BANQUE DU PEUPLE . MONTREAL." Very thick coin and milled edge.

72. C. Obv. Boquet. 1 Rose and bud, 7 leaves, 1 thistle, 2 shamrocks, 1 large leaf and 1 head wheat, to right; 1 rose 2 buds, 1 thistle with 2 leaves, (one of which turns over the centre,) 2 shamrocks, 2 heads wheat with small blades, to left; large open and slender bow and one ribbon to left, and one curved ribbon to right. "＊ TRADE & AGRICULTURE ＊ LOWER CANADA." Rev. Wreath composed of 21 laurel leaves to left, and 27 long slender leaves to right, bound by a double bow to right and left, 2 short ribbons below. In centre of wreath " UN SOU." Inscription, " BANK OF MONTREAL TOKEN." Edge plain. Plate 6, Fig 7.

73. C. Obv. Same as No. 72, but no asterisks before or after inscription. Rev. Wreath of 20 laurel leaves to left, and 30 leaves as in No. 72 to right, connected by a double bow. Stems of wreath touch letters " N " and " E " in Montreal. " UN SOUS," in centre. " BANK TOKEN MONTREAL." Edge milled.

74. C. Obv. Same as No. 73. Rev. Similar wreath to No. 73, but having 21 leaves to left and 25 to right; double bow. Stems of wreath do not extend so far downwards, and are much lighter. " BANK OF MONTREAL TOKEN."

75. C. Obv. Boquet. Large maple leaf, thistle, 1 bunch of 4 and 1 single blade wheat, and 1 head of wheat, bent downwards towards thistle; to right; 1 rose and bud, 4 leaves, 3 leaved sprig of shamrock, 2 blades and 1 head of wheat inclined downwards to left; large open bow and ribbon to right and left. "• AGRICULTURE & COMMERCE • BAS—CANADA." Rev. Wreath of 5 maple leaves, 2 on right, and left turned upwards, that on top inclined downwards to left; in centre, "UN SOU." Outside of wreath, to right a small head wearing a Swiss liberty cap; to left a large five pointed star. "BANQUE DU PEUPLE MONTREAL." Milled edge. Scarce. Plate 7, Fig. 5.

This token is what is commonly known as the *Rebellion* token. It is supposed to have been issued in 1837, the liberty cap and star having reference to the struggle then going on. Scarce in good condition.

76. C. Obv. Boquet. 1 Rose, 4 leaves, 4 shamrocks, and 1 head of wheat to right; 2 thistles, 3 shamrocks, 1 blade and 1 head of wheat, 3 leaves as in No. 39, to left; on top, 3 blades wheat; open slender bow to left, 1 ribbon to right. Same inscription as in No. 48. Rev. Same as No. 39.

A specimen of this coin in possession of Mr. E. Groh, of New York, is struck in German Silver.

77. C. Obv. Boquet. Rose, Thistle, Shamrock, and head of Wheat, to right and left. "• TRADE & AGRICULTURE • LOWER CANADA." Between the inscription are 2 large five-pointed stars. Rev. Wreath composed of 11 laurel leaves and 4 sprigs, to left; and 15 long slender leaves as in No. 72, to right. Wreath bound by 2 very large open bows, twisted like a rope to right and left, with two ends hanging downwards over front of wreath. In centre of wreath, "½ PENNY." Inscription, "BANK TOKEN MONTREAL." Edge plain. Very rare. Plate 6, Fig. 5.

78. C. Obv. Boquet entirely different in form from any other specimen, the flowers being very delicate. "AGRICULTURE & COMMERCE BAS CANADA." Rev. Open wreath with very slender stems, and 18 leaves, with sprigs between. No bow but a small ribbon over the front of wreath. No dot over "o" in Sou. Stems of wreath almost touch letters "N" and "E" in Montreal. Plate 6, Fig. 6.

The dies of this coin, were found in the cellar of an old building on Notre Dame Street, occupied by Dr. Picault, and are now in the Cabinet of the *Numismatic and Antiquarian Society* of Montreal. They are well executed, but not deeply cut, and are much larger than the usual *Un Sou* specimens, which probably is the reason they have never been used. No coins have ever been met with, struck from these dies, with the exception of 4 or 5 proofs in lead, and about 12 in copper.

79. Brass. Obv. Very open and slender boquet. 1 Rose, 4 leaves, 4 shamrocks, to right; 2 thistles, with 2 small leaves attached, 3 shamrocks, one of which turns over centre, to left. In centre, a leaf as in No. 39; on top, 2 similar leaves, attached to thistle on left, 2 heads and 2 blades wheat, the latter bending over to right and left The whole bound by a slender bow to left, and ribbon to right. "• AGRICULTURE & COMMERCE • BAS CANADA." Rev. Open wreath of 18 leaves with sprigs between, 9 on each side; no bow, but 2 leaves start upwards to right and left, from centre. "UN SOU," in large open letters, in centre. "TOKEN MONTREAL." Edge plain. Rare. Plate 8, Fig. 1.

80 C. Obv. Boquet. 1 Rose, 6 leaves, 3 shamrocks, to right; 2 thistles, 3 leaves, to left; one of these leaves turns over and forms centre of boquet; on top, in centre, 1 blade of wheat, with head of wheat on either side. "• AGRICULTURE & COMMERCE • BAS-CANADA." The letters are exceedingly rough, and the die is cracked in two places.

Rev. An Eagle supporting a shield, on which an anchor is inscribed, the whole being surrounded by thirteen stars of six points each. " T. DUSEAMAN BUTCHER BELLEVILLE." Between the words " BUTCHER " and " BELLEVILLE," is a large five-pointed star, and between " T." and " BELLEVILLE," is a small star. Edge plain. For reverse see Plate 6, Fig. 8.

This is claimed by Dickenson as a Jersey token. Certainly the reverse is more like an American than a Canadian device, unless the coin was struck during the Rebellion of 1837-38. If this was so, we can easily account for the Eagle and stars, with the emblem of Hope. It must however be admitted that the obverse is Canadian. Taking the coin as it stands, it is a curiosity, American devices on the one side—English Roses and Scotch Thistles on the other—while to complete the medley we have Bas Canada (Lower Canada), whereas Belleville, (supposing it to be the Canadian town,) is situated in Upper Canada or as it is now called the Province of Ontario.

81. C. Obv. Front and side view of same building as No. 30. " BANK OF MONTREAL 1838." Rev. Same as No. 26, but name of Bank on scroll in raised letters, and no date. Edge plain. Plate 1, Fig. 1.

82. C. Obv. Same as No. 81. Rev. do., do. "HALF PENNY."

83, C. Obv. Same as No. 81. Date, " 1839." Rev. do., do.

84. C. Obv. Same as No. 81. Date, " 1839." Rev. Same as No. 82.

These four coins are very rare, Nos. 81 and 82 particularly so. A specimen of No. 82, supposed to be the only one in the city, was sold in the collection of Mr. Hall, in March, 1868, for $10, the agent who purchased having authority to pay $20 for it.

85. C. Obv. " CANADA 1841." Rev. Same as No. 21.

86. C. Obv. Same as No. 30.   Rev. Same as No. 26. date. "1842."

87. C. Obv. Same as No. 30.   Rev. Same as No. 26, "HALF PENNY 1842."

These coins, Nos. 86 and 87 also appear bearing date, " 1844."

88. C. Obv. St. George on horseback, to the right, slaying the dragon.   In exergue between two roses, " 1850."   On the ground under the dragon, "R. K & Co. BANK OF UPPER CANADA." Rev. Arms of Upper Canada.   "BANK TOKEN ONE PENNY." Plate 1, Fig. 7.

89. C. Obv. Same as 88.   Rev. do., do. " HALF PENNY."

These coins are well executed.   The device on the obverse is copied from Pistruccis crown piece.   They also occur of the dates " 1852," " 1854" and " 1857."

90. C. Obv. Same as No. 26.   Rev. Arms of Quebec, " QUEBEC BANK TOKEN 1852 ONE PENNY."   Plate 1, Fig. 6.

91. C. Obv. Same as No. 26.   Rev. Same as No. 90, "HALF PENNY."

92. C. Obv. Within a beaded circle, Head of Victoria to left, laureated, " VICTORIA DEI GRATIA CANADA."   Rev. Within a wreath of Maple leaves, in a beaded circle, " ONE CENT 1858." Scarce.   Plate 6, Fig. 4.

93. C. Obv. Same as No. 89.   Rev. do., do., date, " 1859."

The head on these coins, and indeed the whole obverse was designed for an English coinage, but the inner beaded circle not being approved the design was rejected.   The inner circle, very rarely seen on coins of the present day was copied by desire of the master of the Mint, from the bronze coinage, then recently issued by the Emperor Napoleon III.—*Rev. H. Christmas, Vol. II, p.* 201.

PLATE VI

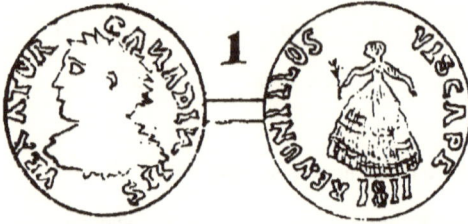

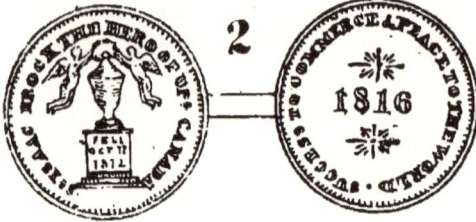

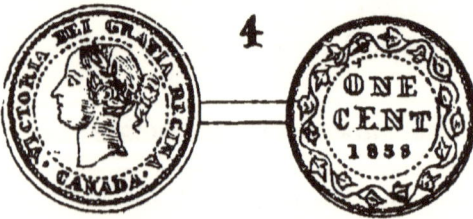

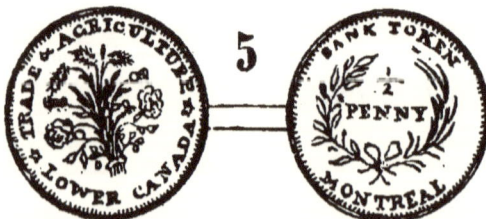

94. C. Obv. A ship under sail to right. Rev. Within a circle of cordage, " R. W. OWEN, MONTREAL ROPERY." Edge engrailed. Very rare. Plate 5, Fig. 5.

No specimen of this coin has been met with in this city.

95. C. Obv. Same head and beaded circle as on No. 92. Inscription, " DOMINION OF CANADA PROVINCE OF QUEBEC." Rev. Within a beaded circla, in 5 lines, " USE | DEVINS' | VEGETABLE | WORM | PASTILLES | JULY 1ST | 1867." Outside of circle, " DEVINS & BOLTON * DRUGGISTS, MONTREAL."

No specimen of this token has as yet been issued. They were ordered (by the firm whose name they bear,) from Birmingham, but upon their arrival in Canada, were seized by the authorities: the *New Currency Act* (a copy of which will be found in the work,) forbidding the manufacture or importation of coins or tokens. The token is well executed, and is the same size as the Canada Cent, No. 92, and would doubtless pass through a number of hands as such, without the mistake being discovered. The description is taken from the proof sent out to Messrs. Devins & Bolton for approval.

MISCELLANEOUS.

In the years 1822 and 1823 an attempt seems to have been made to institute an uniform coinage for the British colonies, on the decimal system, and coins were struck of the value of 1 and 2 cents, but were never circulated. These are seldom found except as proofs, and are exceedingly rare. We give in Nos. 1 and 2 a description of these coins.

1. C. Obv. Bust of George IV. to left, laureated and draped. " GEOR: IV: D: G: BRI: REX." Rev. In a wreath of oak leaves, "$\frac{1}{50}$ DOLLAR COLONIAL 1823."

2. C. Obv. Same as No. 1. Rev. do., do. "$\frac{1}{100}$ DOLLAR."

3. C. Obv. Locomotive. " MONTREAL & LACHINE RAILROAD COMPANY." Rev. Beaver beside water, trunk of tree with two branches in background. " THIRD CLASS." These checks have a round hole in centre. Plate 1, Fig. 8.

When these tickets or checks were imported, this Railroad connected the city of Montreal and the village of Lachine, distant nine miles. The principal portion of the passengers, were the Indians and Squaws from Caughnawaga, (on the opposite side of the St. Lawrence,) and the men employed upon the Canal then building. It became necessary to secure something more lasting than the ordinary ticket, and accordingly a large supply of these were procured from Birmingham. The Conductor carried them strung up on a piece of wire, which accounts for the hole in centre. These are becoming scarce, as the balance remaining in the hands of the Champlain and St. Lawrence Railway Company, were melted at St. Lamberts, in September, 1862, thus leaving a comparatively small number in circulation.

4. C. Obv. Man ploughing with two oxen. "SPEED THE PLOUGH HALF PENNY TOKEN." Rev. Man threshing grain. "NO LABOUR NO BREAD."

5. C. Obv. Wreath in half circle. "PERSONNE." Rev. "DE L'ISLE DE MONTRÉAL À RFPENTIGUY ON LACHESNAYE." Plate 7, Fig. 1.

6. C. Obv. Same as No. 5. Rev. "DE REPENTIGUY À L'ISLE DE MONTRÉAL ON LACHESNAYE."

7. C. Obv. Same as No. 5. Rev. "DE LACHESNAYE À L'ISLE DE MONTRÉAL ON REPENTIGUY."

8. C. Obv. "CHEVAL." Scroll above and below. Rev. Same as No. 5. Plate 7, Fig. 2.

9. C. Obv. Same as No. 8. Rev. Same as No. 6.

10. C. Obv. Same as No. 8. Rev. Same as No. 7.

11. C. Obv. "CALECHE." Above and below a rose with three leaves on either side. Rev. Same as No. 5.

12. C. Obv. Same as No. 11. Rev. Same as No. 6. Plate 7, Fig. 4.

13. C. Obv. Same as No. 11. Rev. Same as No. 7.

14. C. Obv. "CHARRETTE." Above and below two sprigs laurel with bow. Rev. Same as No. 5.

15. C. Obv. Same as No. 14. Rev. Same as No. 6.

16. C. Obv. Same as No. 14. Rev. Same as No. 7. Clipped. Plate 7, Fig. 3.

Nos. 5 to 16 inclusive, were used as Toll Checks for crossing the bridge, known as the *Porteous Bridge*, which was erected in 1808, to connect the Island of Repentiguy with that of Montreal. The bridge was destroyed many years ago. These checks are very rare, a good specimen commanding from $1 to $3.

17. C. Obv. "FISHERIES AND AGRICULTURE." Rev. "ONE CENT 1855." Edge plain.

DOUBTFUL.

1. C. Obv. Bust (to left,) in civilian dress " BRITISH COLONIES." Rev. Female figure to left, seated on a bale of merchandise. Right arm extended and holding a sprig of flowers, left hand resting on the bale. " TO FACILITATE TRADE 1825." Edge plain. Plate 8, Fig. 3.

2. C. Obv. Bust of George III. (to right,) laureated and draped, within a circle, or wreath composed of oak leaves and acorns. No inscription. Rev. Female figure as on No. 1 ; right hand holds a pair of scales; left arm supports a cornucopia ; to left, in distance, a small vessel under sail. " HALF PENNY TOKEN 1812." Edge milled.

3. C. Obv. Female figure as on reverse of No. 1; left hand holding Mercury's wand, vessel to left, in distance. " TRADE & NAVIGATION." In exergue, "1812." Rev. Within a circle, (single line,) " HALF | PENNY | TOKEN " in three lines; outside of circle, " PURE COPPER PREFERABLE TO PAPER." Edge engrailed. Plate 8, Fig. 4.

4. C. Obv. Within a circle, a ship (to left), with topsails set, masts lean towards left. "TRADE & NAVIGATION 1812." Rev. Same as No. 3, but with circle of double lines. Edge plain.

5. C. Same as No. 3, date "1813."

6. C. Obv. Ship in full sail, (to right); flag on stern of ship bears St. George's Cross. " FOR GENERAL ACCOMMODATION." Rev. Same as No. 3.

7. C. Obv. Ship in full sail, to right. No inscription. Rev. Female figure, (as on No. 2). " HALF PENNY TOKEN." Milled edge.

PLATE VII

1

2

4

3

5

6

8

7

8. Brass. Obv. Female figure (Hibernia,) seated, to left and resting upon a harp, at bottom of which appears a single leaf of shamrock. "ONE HALF PENNY TOKEN 1820." Rev. Frigate under sail, to left. "TRADE AND NAVIGATION." Edge plain,

9. C. Obv. A monogram. "R. H." within a wreath composed of oak leaves and acorns. Rev. Within a circle, a vessel as on No. 4. "HALF PENNY TOKEN 1814." Edge plain.

10. C. Obv. Same as No. 9. Rev. Same as No· 9, "ONE PENNY TOKEN 1814."

11. C. Obv. Bust of George III. to right, laureated and draped. "GENUINE BRITISH COPPER 1815." Rev. Female seated as on No 1; left hand holding a trident, an oval shield by her side, bearing upon it a Union Jack. "HALF PENNY." Milled edge.

12. C. Obv. A wreath composed of oak and shamrock leaves, within which stands a man with right hand uplifted and bearing a club ; left hand hanging downward and holding a triple leaved sprig of shamrock. No inscription· Rev. "PURE | COPPER | PREFER-ABLE | TO PAPER," in four lines. Milled edge.

13. C. Obv. Vessel under sail, to right. No inscription, Rev. "SHIPS | COLONIES | & | COMMERCE," in four lines. Edge plain.

There are some 7 or 8 varieties of this token, the difference being in the arrangement of the sails—the size of the flag at the stern,—or, size and form of letters on the reverse, some of which are small and close, others large and open.

14. C. Obv. A spread eagle, holding in the dexter claw a sprig of olive, in sinister claw, four arrows crossed. "HALF PENNY TOKEN 1813." The tail of the eagle divides the date, "18—13." Rev. Within a circle or wreath of oak leaves and acorns, is seated a female as on No. 11. Edge engrailed.

15. C. Same as No. 14, date "1814,"

16. C. Obv. Same as No. 14, but eagle higher up on the coin, leaving the date "1815 " below the tail. Rev. Same as No. 14, but wreath much finer and female figure more slender. Edge engrailed. Plate 8, Fig. 6.

17. C. Obv. Same as reverse of No. 2. Bale inscribed "s. j. & c." No inscription. Rev. Frigate under sail, to right. No inscription. Edge plain.

18. C. Obv. Same as No. 17, date " 1815." Rev. do., do.

19. C. Obv. Bust in military dress, to right. No inscription. Rev. Female figure to left, seated on a bale of merchandise, on which her right hand is resting, the left being extended and holding a pair of scales. "TO FACILITATE TRADE." Head of figure close to second letter " I " in Facilitate; the foot touches letter " E " in Trade. Edge plain.

There are several varieties of this coin in circulation, bearing the same bust for obverse, the reverse being same as Nos. 11 or 19. They are also different in size, some being about the same as the American half cent.

20. C. Obv. Small bust of George III. to right, laureated and draped. " HALF PENNY TOKEN 1815." Rev. Ship under sail, to right. " SUCCESS TO NAVIGATION & TRADE." Edge plain.

21. C. Obv. Bust of George III. as on No. 20. No inscription. Rev. Female figure as on No. 11. " GENUINE BRITISH COPPER." Edge plain.

22. C. Obv. Bust as on No. 20. No inscription, but date "1820." below bust. Rev. Same figure as No. 11. No inscription.

23. Brass. Obv. Laureated bust in armour, to left. No inscription. Rev. A harp with 9 strings, date "1820" below. Edge plain.

24. Brass. Same bust and harp as on obverse and reverse of No. 23, but has evidently been produced by some inferior workman. The leaves in laurels on the head of bust are more open, and the branch very slender. The forehead is exceedingly low, and the details of the hair poorly executed. The harp has 10 strings, and the wings of the angel on it, are clumsy in appearance.

25. C. Obv. Bust of George III., to right; laureated and draped, within a circle of oak leaves and acorns. No inscription. Rev. Female figure as in No. 11. "HALFPENNY TOKEN 1812." Plain edge. Plate 8, Fig. 5.

26. Brass. Obv. Same as No. 25; leaves on outside of circle are larger than those on the inside. The bust not so well executed. Rev. Same as No. 25.

There are four other varieties of this coin in brass. The difference consisting in the number of leaves in the circle or wreath on the obverse, or in the position of the figure on the reverse. By inspecting the coins the difference is quite easily observed, but the details are so minute as to preclude the possibility of accurately describing them.

27. C. Obv. Female figure as in No. 8. "NORTH AMERICAN TOKEN 1781." Rev. Two masted vessel to left, with four sails set, and flag at stern. "COMMERCE."

This is generally classed among the early American Tokens. In "Prime's" work on Coins and Tokens, he places it (on pages 245-6) in his list of Colonial and Rare American Coins, and values it at 25 cents, certainly not a high price, but still it is more than it would command in Canada where scores may be procured at any time, and in good condition, for two or three cents each.

28. C. Obv. Very large and coarse bust to right. "GEORICVS III, VIS." Rev. Coarsely executed figure of female seated, to left, and holding in her hand a leaf similar to (and probably intended as) a shamrock. "BRITT." round left side of coin. Edge plain.

There are two or three varieties of No. 28 remarkable for nothing but their coarse workmanship and the very poor condition in which they are generally found.

29. Brass. Obv. Vessel under sail to right. "SHIPS, COLONIES & COMMERCE 1815." Rev. "ONE | HALFPENNY | TOKEN." Edge plain.

30. Brass. Obv. Same as No. 29. Rev. "FOR | PUBLICK | ACCOMMODATION." Edge plain. Scarce.

The following coins, No. 31 to No. 46, inclusive, were until the past few years, very plentiful in Canada, and collectors have classed them as Canadian. The following extracts from a letter lately received from a gentleman in this city, will give some information about these and other tokens. He says:

"When I first went into business in 1818, we had a great many English half-pence in circulation, and in Upper Canada they had a flood of light tokens, called *Brock Coppers*, (Nos. 9, 10 and 11 on page 22). When other coins became scarce, these got into circulation here until they became so plentiful that everybody rejected them. Next came the importation of English tokens of pure copper about the weight of half-pence. These were of every variety, many bearing the bust of Wellington. From 1825 to 1828, there appeared large numbers of light copper coins, which circulated freely for a few months, and then were suddenly refused. I have known retail grocers have barrels full in their stores. This state of things lasted for some time. The decision as to what should or should not circulate rested in the determination of the old women who sold upon the markets. Their voice was law in the matter. What they took was current everywhere, and what they refused nobody would take. Unfortunately they were whimsical in their decision. What they called good one week, they would call bad the next, and *vice versa*. As we had hundreds of varieties, it was not an easy task to keep posted upon the " copper " market. Where these coins came from nobody seemed to know, as they had all an old appearance."

31. C. Obv. Bust of Wellington to left, laureated and draped. " J. FARRES," on bottom of bust. " WELLINGTON & VICTORY 1814." Rev. Female figure seated on a rock ; right arm extended and holding an olive branch ; left hand holding a spear. Leaning against the rock is a round shield with a harp inscribed upon it ; to left, in distance, is a ship ; on the ground are letters " I. P. F. ;" in exergue " 1816." Above the figure " EDWD BEWLY." Edge engrailed. This is of the size of a penny token.

32. C. Obv. Bust of Wellington in military dress, to right. " VIMIERA, TALAVERA, BUSACO, BADAJOZ, SALAMANCA." Rev. Figure (Cossack) mounted on horseback, and bearing a gun and spear. Above "COSSACK," below " PENNY TOKEN." Edge engrailed. Scarce.

33. C. Obv. Same bust as No. 32, but finer in details. Same inscription. Rev. Female figure as on No. 11, with a vessel in the distance to left. " ONE PENNY TOKEN 1813." One point of trident touches " o " in Token. Edge engrailed.

34. C. Obv. Laureated bust of Wellington in military dress, immediately below the bust are 2 sprigs of laurel of 9 leaves each, which extend upwards, about one-third round the coin to right and left. " FIELD MARSHAL WELLINGTON." Rev. Similar figure to No. 33, but better executed. The fork of trident touches letter " K " in Token. Immediately below the figure are sprigs of laurel same as on the obverse. " ONE PENNY TOKEN." Edge engrailed.

This has been struck over some other coin, and in some specimens the letters of the original die are distinct in different parts. The coin from which we take this description has the letter "N" quite legible on the side of the head, as well as portions of letters appearing on the inscription, both on obverse and reverse.

35. C. Obv. Same as No. 13. Rev. "WELLINGTON | WATER-LOO | 1815," in three lines. Edge plain.

36. C. Obv. Laureated bust of Wellington to left, in military dress. A very delicate wreath of 13 leaves on either side. No inscription. Rev. Female figure to left, seated on a square bale of Goods; the right hand extended and holding a pair of scales, while the left supports a straight staff or wand; a small ship to left in distance. "TRADE & COMMERCE 1811." The wreath on obverse and inscription on reverse are very poor. Edge plain.

37. C. Obv. Bust of Wellington to right laureated and draped. "MARQUIS WELLINGTON 1813." Rev. Figure as on No. 11, but supporting a wand instead of a trident. Small vessel to left, in distance. Edge engrailed.

38. C. Obv. Bust of Wellington to left, laureated and in military dress. Laurels bound by small bow with two strings hanging downwards. "THE ILLUSTRIOUS WELLINGTON." Rev. A crowned harp. "WATERLOO HALF PENNY 1816." Edge milled. Plate 8, Fig. 2.

39. C. Obv. Similar bust to No. 38, nose much sharper, lips open and somewhat protruding. "WELLINGTON | HALF PENNY | TOKEN." Rev. Figure as on No. 11, ship to left, in distance; 2 sprigs of oak (17 leaves and 7 acorns each,) start from each side of ground below figure. In exergue "1814." Edge engrailed.

40. C. Obv. Similar to No. 38, no bow to laurel on bust, and but one string hanging down. Same inscription. Rev. Same as No. 39 but no ship. Edge engrailed.

PLATE VIII.

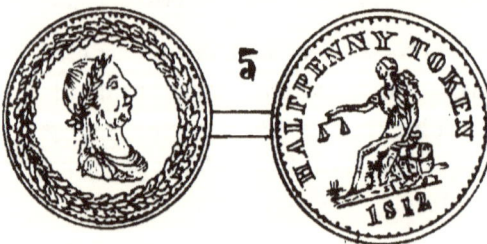

41. C. Obv. Bust as on No. 38, otherwise same as No. 34, Rev. Figure as on No. 11, with ship to left. " HALF PENNY TOKEN 1813." Edge engrailed.

42. C. Obv. Bust as on No. 38, below which are 2 sprigs of laurel (5 leaves on each). " FIELD MARSHAL WELLINGTON." Rev. Figure as on No. 11, below which are 2 sprigs of laurel, (10 leaves on each). " HALF PENNY TOKEN." Edge plain.

43. C. Obv. Naked bust of Wellington. Same inscription as No. 42 Rev. Crowned harp. " HIBERNIA 1805." Edge milled.

44. C. Obv. Bust as on No. 38. " HISPANIAM ET LVSITANIAM RESTITVIT WELLINGTON." Rev. Within a circle in eight lines, " CUIDAD | RODRIGO | JAN. 19, 1812 | BADAJOZ | APRIL 2, 1812." Outside of circle, " VIMIERA AUG. 21, 1808. TALAVERA JULY 28 1809. ALMEIDA MAY 5, 1811." Edge milled.

45. C. Obv. Nearly the same as No. 44. Letters somewhat larger Rev. A circle, outside of which is same inscription as No. 44; inside of circle and running parallel with it, " CUIDAD RODRIGO JAN 19, 1812. BADAJOZ APRIL 2. 1812." In centre of these, in 8 lines, (the lower one being a semi-circle.) " SALAMANCA | JULY 22. 1812. | MADRID | AUG. 12. 1812. | ST. SEBASTIAN | SEPT. 8. 1813. | PAMPLUNO | OCT. 31, 1813." Edge milled. Scarce.

46. C. Obv. Same as No. 44. Rev. A circle, outside of which is same inscription as No. 44. Inside of circle, in 9 lines, (the lower line a semi-circle, " CUIDAD | RODRIGO | JAN. 19. 1812. | BADAJOZ | APRIL 2. 1812. | SALAMANCA | JULY. 22. 1812. | MADRID | AUG. 12. 1812." Edge plain.

47. C. Obv. Bust in uniform, to right; below are 2 sprigs of laurel, (9 leaves on each,) bound by a ribbon with double bow. " VICTORIA NOBIS EST." Rev. Figure as on No. 11, with ship to left, in the distance. In exergue, 2 sprigs laurel, (5 leaves on each). " HALF PENNY TOKEN." Edge engrailed. Plate 8, Fig. 8, shows the obverse.

48. C. Obv. Same as No. 2, but the wreath is open at top and bottom, and between the lower ends is the date, " 1812." Rev. Same as No. 2. " ONE PENNY TOKEN."

49. C. Same as No. 48, date "1813."

50. C. Obv. Same as No. 3, date. " 1813." Rev. Same as No. 3 "ONE PENNY TOKEN." Edge engrailed.

51. C. Obv. Same as No. 3, date "1814." Rev. Same as No. 50.

52. C. Obv. Bust of George III., laureated and draped, to left. " PURE COPPER PREFERABLE TO PAPER." Rev. Same as obverse of No. 3, date "1838." Edge plain.

53. C. Obv. Laureated and draped bust of George III., to right. " HALF PENNY TOKEN 1814." Rev. Frigate in full sail, to right. " FOR THE CONVENIENCE OF TRADE." Edge plain.

54. C. Obv. Ship under sail, to left. " COMMERCE." Rev. In centre, " 1828 "— on top, " ONE FARTHING "—below, " TOKEN." Milled edge.

55. C. Obv. " HAMILTON RETAILERS TOKEN." Rev. " ONE FARTHING 1814." Edge plain.

MEDALS.

The sizes are according to the American Scale of one-sixteenth of an inch.

1. Obv. Head of Louis, to right. "LVDOVICVS . MAGNVS . REX CHRISTIANISSIMVS." Rev. France seated on a rock, with flags, a beaver and a river god. "FRANCIA IN NOVO ORBE VICTRIX;" in exergue, "KEBECA LIBERATA, MDCXC. Very rare. Size 32.

In 1690, the French Governor of Canada, (Count de Frontenac,) organized three expeditions, to invade the British settlements, (now the United States). The first expedition surprised Corlaer or Schenectady, and massacred its inhabitants; the second demolished the village of Salmon Falls in New Hampshire, and in returning fell in with the 3rd Division, and joining forces they gained possession of the fortified village of Kaskabé in Maine. The New Englanders resolved on reprisals, and besides sending out a small squadron which took Port Royal, they planned two expeditions against Canada; one by sea from Boston, against Quebec; the other by land from New York against Montreal. The latter failed from want of stores, &c., and fell back without accomplishing anything. The Naval force took several small posts on the lower St. Lawrence, and finally reached Quebec. The Count de Frontenac refused to surrender, and Sir Wm. Phipps, who commanded the English fleet, landed about 1500 troops and some field pieces, but through the courage and zeal of the French, he was compelled to desist from his attempts. Considering the enterprise hopeless, he re-embarked his soldiers, leaving his cannon in the hands of the enemy. The French King on receiving intelligence of the victory, caused this medal to be struck in commemoration of the event.

2. Obv. Laureated bust of George II. to left, in armour. "GEORGIVS II. REX." Rev. In centre, Arms; a shield bearing an inverted *Fleur de Lys*, surrounded by a garter, inscribed, "PERFIDIA EVERSA." The whole supported by a crowned lion to left, and an unicorn to right. Ribbon below inscribed, "W. PITT | AUSP: GEO: II. | PR: MI:." Immediately over the arms, "HAWKE QUIBERON NOV. 20;" above which in a shield, "QUEBEC | WOLFE | MONKⁿ TOWNSᴅ | SEP. 13 & 18." Under the Arms, "MDCCLIX;" below which in a shield, "MINDEN | FERDINAND | AUG. 1." On right side of Arms, "CROWN POINT | AMHERST AUG. 4, LAGOS | BOSCOWAN |

AUG. 19;" to left, "GUADALOUPE | BARRING^N MOORE | MAY 1 | ;
NIAGARA | IOHNSON | IULY 25." Rare. Size 26.

3. Obv. Britannia seated in a chariot drawn by a lion, and supported by Liberty and Justice. The ground upon which the figures
stand is studded with Fleur de Lys. On a ribbon is inscribed,
"FŒDUS—INVECTUM." In a straight line below, "MDCCLVIII."
Round the medal in two lines, "SENEGAL MAI 2. S^T MALOS IUN.
16. CHERBOURG AU. 16. LOUISBOURG IUL. 27. FRONTE₀ AUG.
27. DUQUESNE NOV. 24. GORREE DE. 29. | MARSH. MASON,
MARLBRO. | HOW, | BOSCAWEN. | AMHERST, | BRADSTREET. | FOR-
BES, | KEPPEL." Rev. Same as No. 1. Rare. Size 26.

4. Obv. Same as reverse of No. 2. Rev. Same as reverse of No. 3.
Size 26.

5. Obv. Same as No. 2. Rev. Same as obverse of No. 3.

6. Obv. A Globe with a soldier and a sailor pointing to Canada;
above, Fame blowing a trumpet; below, prostrate figure of France.
Rev. Naval scene, with forts, &c. "LOVISBOVRG TAKEN MDCCLVIII."
Rare. Size 28.

7. Obv. Head of Britannia. "O FAIR BRITANNIA HAIL."
Rev. Victory marching &c. Same inscription as No. 6. Very Rare
Size 27.

8. Obv. Similar to No. 6. Rev. Victory standing on the prow of
a vessel and holding a crown. Same inscription as No. 6. Very
rare. Size 27.

9. Obv. Head of Britannia. "SAUNDERS WOLFE &C." Rev.
Victory marching. Same inscription as Nos. 6, 7 and 8, but different style. Rare. Size 27.

10. Obv. Bust of Admiral Boscowan. "ADM_L BOSCOWAN TOOK CAPE BRETON." Rev. A fort, ships, &c. "LOUISBOURG . JUL 26 1758." Rare. Size 25.

11. Obv. Bust of General Wolfe, to right. "JACOBUS WOLFE ANGLUS." Rev, In centre, an urn upon a pedestal, surrounded by military trophies. "IN VICTORI CÆSVS QUEBECÆ SEP^T XIII., MDCCLIX PRO PATRIA." Very rare. Size 25.

12. Obv. Head between a trident and standard crossed, a wreath binding them. Under the trident, "SAVNDERS;" under the standard, "WOLFE." Rev. Victory crowning a trophy, a captive bound. QVEBEC TAKEN, MDCCLIX." Very rare. Size 27.

13. Obv. A laureated male figure, reclining with right arm on prow of a Roman galley, the left holding a rudder; in background, a Roman standard, with wreath of laurel encircling the name of "AMHERST," the whole surmounted by a lion; below in exergue, a shield, bow, battle-axe and quiver of arrows. "CONQVEST OF CANADA COMPLEATED." Rev. A female seated weeping under a pine tree; before her, a shield battle-axe and sword; behind, an eagle seated on a rock; in exergue, "SOC. PROMOTING ARTS AND COMMERCE;" above the figure, "MONTREAL TAKEN MDCCLX." Rare. Size 23.

14. Obv. Bust of George II. to left. "GEORGIUS II. REX." Rev. Same figure as on No. 13. "CANADA SUBDUED MDCCLX." Rare. Size 24.

15. Obv. A representation of the Crucifixion, with a Roman soldier to right, and a female figure to left. "JESUS ABREUVE DE FIEL ET DE VINAIGRE AYEZ PITIÉ DE NOUS;" in exergue, "JE SERAI TOUJOUR FIDÈLE À MA PROMESSE." Rev. A representation of John the Baptist bearing a cross, to which is attached a ribbon, bearing the inscription "TEMPERANCE." In exergue, 2 sprigs of maple 6 leaves on each, in centre of which is a beaver, above the beaver is name of die-sinker. "DAVIS BIRM." Inscription, "IL NE BOIRA NI VIN NI AUCUNE LIQUEUR ENIVRANTE." Size 25.

16. Obv. Arms of the Board of Arts. "Lᴱ CANADA BOARD OF ARTS & MANUFACTURES. CHAMBRE DES ARTS ET MANUFACTURES BAS CANADA." Rev. A wreath of Maple leaves, between tops of wreath is Prince of Wales feather, with motto, "ICH DIEN." In centre of wreath in 8 lines, "EXHIBITION OF | CANADIAN INDUSTRY | OPENING OF | VICTORIA BRIDGE | BY H. R. H. | PRINCE OF WALES | MONTREAL | 1860." Size 24.

17. Obv. Same as on No. 16. Rev. Wreath of maple leaves, within which is inscribed in a circle, LOWER CANADA PROVINCIAL EXHIBITION." In centre, in two lines, "HONORIS | CAUSA," with space below to insert a name. Size 24.

These two medals were engraved by J. S. Wyon of London, for the Lower Canada Board of Arts. No. 17, is the medal awarded at the regular exhibitions of the Society. It is in Bronze and Silver. Exhibitors awarded a prize of $5 and upwards, have the option of taking a bronze medal, and for $10 and upwards, a silver one. On the occasion of the visit of the Prince of Wales to Canada, an Exhibition was held in the Crystal Palace, (a building erected for the purpose), and which was by far the most successful ever held. It had previously been decided that all medals awarded on this occasion should be specially prepared, and accordingly a new reverse die was executed for them. Only a sufficient number of medals were struck to supply the Exhibitors to whom they were awarded. Consequently the medal is rarely found in the possession of any others, the exceptional cases being when persons took the medal, but not attaching much value to it, have sold it to a collector.

18. Obv. A full face bust of the Prince of Wales in uniform, as Colonel of the 100th Canadian Regiment. "H. R. H. THE PRINCE OF 'WALES." Immediately below the bust, "BORN 9 NOV. 1841." Rev. A wreath of laurel leaves, joined by a Prince of Wales feather with motto, "ICH DIEN." In centre of wreath in 8 lines, "TO |

COMMEMORATE | THE VISIT OF | ALBERT EDWARD | PRINCE OF
WALES | TO | CANADA | 1860." Size 26.

19. Obv. Same as No. 18. Rev. A view of Victoria Bridge.
" VICTORIA BRIDGE MONTREAL, OPENED BY THE PRINCE OF
WALES 1860." Size 26.

20. Obv. Head of the Prince to left, below which in small letters

" J. S. WYON SC." Inscription, "ALBERT EDWARD PRINCE OF WALES." Rev. In centre, a large Prince of Wales feather, partially surrounded by a wreath of Maple leaves over which is laid a ribbon inscribed, " WELCOME | WELCOME | WELCOME." Inscription, "VISITED CANADA AND INAUGURATED THE VICTORIA BRIDGE 1860." Size 30.

This beautiful medal was executed for the Grand Trunk Railway Company of Canada, and being very sparingly distributed, is consequently extremely rare. At the opening of the Bridge a copy in gold was given to the Prince of Wales, and each member of his staff received one in silver.

21. Obv. Draped bust of Trevithick, to left. " GRAND TRUNK RAILWAY COMPANY OF CANADA " Immediately behind the bust, in two lines, appears the name "RICHARD | TREVITHICK." Below the bust, " J. S. WYON SC." Rev. Six ornamented oblong shields. The centre one being blank, the others are inscribed as follows: " PRESENTED BY THE | DIRECTORS | TO | .... | FOR | GENERAL EFFICIENCY AND GOOD CONDUCT DURING THE YEAR." Behind the shields appear the English Union Jack and American Flag. The whole surrounded by a wreath of maple leaves, with 5 stars above and 3 below. On edge of medal in sunk letters, " F. H TREVITHICK LOCO. SUPERINT^T." Size 28.

The object for which this medal was struck, is explained by the inscriptions. It was procured during the time Mr. Trevithick held the position of Locomotive Superintendant, and was given to Engineers who by good conduct merited the honor.

22. Obv. In centre, extending entirely across the face of the medal
is a view of Victoria Bridge, with Mount Royal in the distance, a
raft of lumber, and steamer in foreground. Below, " THE VICTORIA
BRIDGE, MONTREAL, | THE GREATEST WORK OF | ENGINEERING
SKILL | IN THE WORLD, | PUBLICLY INAGURATED | AND OPENED
IN | 1860. | GRAND TRUNK RAILWAY OF CANADA." Above the
Bridge, Arms, as follows: in centre, Arms of the City of Montreal,
surmounted by a beaver, an Indian on each side, the whole supported
by a lion to left, and unicorn to right, seated on scrolls, with Rose,
Thistle, &c., by side. Ribbons inscribed, " ROSS, STEPHENSON."
Above the Arms, " THE VICTORIA BRIDGE MEDAL." Rev. On
top, Royal Arms of England; to right and left, small circular shields
with sprigs of Rose and Thistle; that to right having a bust in uniform, and inscribed, " PRINCE ALBERT;" that to the left, crowned
bust, " QUEEN VICTORIA." At the bottom, similar shield upon a
Prince of Wales feather, the tops of feather shewing above the shield,
and the ribbon with inscription " ICH DIEN," below. To right of
shield, a beaver; to left a sprig of shamrock. On this shield, a full
face bust in uniform. " PRINCE OF WALES." In centre, in 14 lines
" THE VICTORIA BRIDGE | CONSISTS OF 23 SPANS | 242 F_T EACH

| AND 1 IN CENTRE 330 F^T | WITH A LONG ABUTMENT | ON EACH BANK OF THE RIVER | THE TUBES ARE IRON | 22 F^T HIGH, 16 F^T WIDE | AND WEIGH 6,000 T^{NS} | SUPPORTED ON 24 PIERS | CONTAINING 250,000 TN^S OF STONE | MEASURING 3,000,000 CUBIC FEET | EXTREME LENGTH 2 MILES | COST $5,000,000." Size 30.

This medal is commonly known as the " Hoffnung" medal from the fact that the dies were prepared to the order of Mr. A. Hoffnung of Montreal, by whom it was designed. It was struck in White Metal, Bronze, Silver and Gold. Those in White Metal met with a very extensive sale, and are consequently plentiful; Bronze copies are scarce, and those in Silver or Gold are rarely met with, but in possession of original subscribers.

The following medals form the series awarded by the McGill College of Montreal:

" In 1860, the sum of £200, presented to the College by H. R. H. the Prince of Wales, was applied to the foundation of a Gold Medal to be called the ' Prince of Wales Gold Medal,' for an honor course in Logic and Mental and Moral Philosophy.

" In 1861, the Chapman gold medal was founded by Henry Chapman, Esq., of Montreal, for an honor course in the Classical Languages and Literature.

" In 1864, the ' Anne Molson Gold Medal,' was founded by Mrs. John Molson, of Belmont Hall, Montreal, for an honor course in Mathematics and Physical Science.

" In the same year the ' Shakespeare Gold Medal,' for an honor course, to comprise and include the works of Shakespeare, and the Literature of England from his time to the time of Addison, both inclusive, and such other accessory subjects as the Corporation may from time to time appoint,—was founded by citizens of Montreal, on occasion of the three hundredth Anniversary of the birth of Shakespeare.

" In the same year, the ' Logan Gold Medal,' for an honor course in Geology and Natural Sciences, was founded by Sir William Edmund Logan, LL.D., F.R.S., F.G.S., &c.

" In 1865, the ' Elizabeth Torrance Gold Medal ' was founded by John Torrance, Esq., of St. Antoine Hall, Montreal, in memory of the late Mrs. John Torrance, for the best student in the graduating class in Law, and more especially for the highest proficiency in Roman Law.

" In the same year the ' Holmes Gold Medal ' was founded by the Medical Faculty, as a memorial of the late Andrew Holmes, Esquire, M.D., LL.D,, late Dean of the Faculty of Medicine, to be given to the best Student in the graduating class in Medicine, who shall undergo a special examination in all the branches, whether Primary or Final.

" In event of their being no candidate for any Medal, or of none of the candidates fulfilling the required conditions, the medal is withheld, and the proceeds of its endowment for the year is devoted to prizes in the subject for which the medal was intended."

23. Obv. Head of Prince of Wales to right; " C. F. CARTER SC."

below; "ALBERTUS EDVARDUS ARTIUM LIBERALIUM FAUTOR CANADA VISA D. 1860." Rev. Arms of the College, on right side of which is a branch of Oak with Acorns; on left a branch of Maple; above "UNIVERSITAS MCGILL;" below "MONTE REGIO." Size 26.

24. Obv. God of Labor engaged in tilling the ground; above " VERE NOVO TERRA COLENDA EST." In exergue "GRANDESCUNT AUCTA LABORE." Rev. A wreath of laurel, between the top leaves of which are the arms of the College, with motto. Inside of wreath, "HENRICUS | CHAPMAN | DONAVIT." On outside " UNIVERSITAS COLEGII MCGILL * MONTE REGIO * * * " Size 26.

25. Obv. Head of Newton to left ; below " J.S & A. B. WYON, SC." At back of head, " NEWTON." Round outer edge, " * SCIENTIS . MATHEMATICIS . ET . PHYSICIS . FELICITER . EXULTIS." Rev. A

wreath of laurels, between the top leaves of which appear the Molson arms (a shield bearing six crescents); in centre, in four lines, " ANNA | MOLSON | DONAVIT | 1864." Outside of wreath, above, " UNIVERSITAS MᶜGILL MONTE REGIO." Below, between two five pointed stars, the motto of the College, " IN DOMINO CONFIDO." Size 28.

26. Obv. Bust of Shakespeare to left, " SHAKSPERE 1564-1616." Rev. An ornamented shield, having on top the Arms of the College, with motto ; at bottom is ribbon extending across and inscribed " FOR ENGLISH LITERATURE." In centre, " SHAKSPERE TERCENTENARY 1864." At corners of shield are scrolls. On outer circle, " MᶜGILL . COLLEGE . MONTREAL." Size 26.

27. Obv. Head of Sir William Logan to left; beneath bust, " J. S. WYON SC;" above, " GULIELMUS E. LOGAN : EQUES." Rev. Wreath

of maple leaves, between tops of which are the College Arms. A ribbon below the shield bears the motto, " IN DOMINE CONFIDO." Within the wreath, in four lines, " UNIVERSITAS | MᶜGILL | MONTE | REGIO." Without the wreath and completely round the medal, " : AD : GEOLOGIAM : ET : SCIENTIAS : NATURALES : EXCOLENDAS : GUL : E : LOGAN : EQ . D : 1864 : " Size 28.

28. Obv. Full face bust of Justinian crowned, and wearing Roman toga. To right of bust, an ancient roll inscribed, " PAN | DEC | TAE | ; to left, a globe surmounted by a cross; "JUSTINIANUS." By side of bust, in small letters, " J. S. & A. B. WYON, SC." Rev. Arms of College at top. From upper parts of shield a ribbon extends completely round the medal ; inside of this ribbon are two palm branches which extend upwards and nearly touch the bottom of the shield. Within the wreath in ten lines, " UNIVERSITAS | MᶜGILL | * * * | PREMIUM | IN | FACULTATE | JURIS | * * * | * * | *" On the ribbon, "AD . NOM : ELIZABETH : TORRANCE : PERPETUAND : MARIT : JOANNES . TORRANCE . INST : 1864." Size 28.

29. Obv. Head of Hippocrates to left; below bust, " C. F. CARTER SCULP." "ΙΠΠΟΚΡΑΤΗΣ" Rev. A wreath of laurels, between the top leaves of which are the Arms of the College, (a crowned shield bearing three doves) below which is a ribbon extending across and connecting tops of wreath, inscribed, " UNIVERSITAS MᶜGILL MONTE

REGIO." In centre of wreath, in three lines, "FACULTAS | MEDI-
CINÆ | DONAVIT | " Outside of wreath in circle, "IN MEMORIAM
ANDREÆ F. HOLMES M.D. L L.D." Size 28.

The following medal was founded by D. Davidson, Esq., and is
given as a premium to the scholars of the High School of Montreal,
connected with the McGill College :

30. Obv. Minerva's Head. "NIL SINE MAGNO LABORE." Rev.
Wreath of laurel, with Arms of McGill College at top. In centre in
six lines " HOC PRÆMIUM | INGENII BENE CULTE | REGIÆ SCHOLÆ |
MONTES REGALIS | DONAVIT D. DAVIDSON | TULET." Size 26.

31. Obv. Bust of Prince of Wales to left. Below the bust in
small letters, "CAQUÉE F. GRAVEUR DE S. M. L'EMPEREUR." Rev.
In eleven lines, " EDUARDUS ALBERTUS | PRINCEPS CAMBRIÆ |
PROVINCIAM CANADENSEM | FAUSTA PRÆSENTIA HONORATAM |
PERLUS TRANS | IN UNAQUAQUE NORMALI SCHOLA | PRÆMIUM IN
SINGOLOS ANNOS | MUNIFICÉ INSTITUIT. A.D. MDCCCLX. I IN ......
SCHOLA | .... MER ET CONS | A.D. 18...... | Size 36.

This medal was founded by the Prince of Wales to commemorate
his visit to Canada, and is presented to students of the Jacques
Cartier Normal School.

32. Obv. Goddess draped, bearing in her right hand, and holding forward a wreath of laurel; her left hangs downwards and holds a palm branch; on either side in straight line " ΜΗ ΑΗΓΟΙ ΣΤΕΦΑΝΟΥΣΑ " Size 25.

This is the Medal of the University of Toronto. Some are in gold and others in silver. The obverse of all the medals of this University is the same. The reverse varies with the name, and the subject in which the medal has been awarded. When given for proficiency in Natural Science it reads, " PROPTER | CHEM . ETC . BOTAN . ETC . | ET GEOLOG . ETC. | FELICITER EXULTAS | " If it were a Classical medal the inscription would be " PROPTER LITT. GRAEC. ET LAT. FELICITER EXCULTAS."

There will shortly be another medal connected with the University, founded by the late Richard Noble Starr, M.D., who by his last will and testament devised certain property for the purpose of founding a medal in the Faculty of Medicine. The design of this medal has not as yet been settled.

33. Obv. A pointed shield, divided into three parts, the upper half having a landscape with cattle; dividing this from two lower compartments is a line inscribed " PRATIQUE AVEC SCIENCE." In lower division to right, a field with agricultural implement; to left

a field with trees in distance and machine for removing stumps in foreground. Above upper corner of the shield are cornucopias with grain hanging down each side of shield. On top, in centre, a beaver with maple leaf behind it. " CHAMBRE D'AGRICULTURE DU BAS CANADA CRÉÉE EN 1852." Rev. Fame blowing a trumpet, which is held by the right hand, while the left is extended and holds two wreaths of laurel. Above " EXPOSITION PROVINCIALE AGRICOLE." At bottom, in very small letters, " CAQUÉ Gᴿ DE L'EMPEREUR." Size 26.

34. Obv. Arms of Masonic Grand Lodge. " GRAND LODGE OF ANCIENT FREE AND ACCEPTED MASONS OF CANADA." Rev. Within a wreath of maple and laurel leaves, " TO COMMEMORATE THE UNION CONSUMMATED 14TH JULY 1858." Size 26.

The dies for this medal are in possession of Hendery & Co. of Montreal. But a very few specimens were struck, there being but one to our knowledge now in this city.

35. Obv. Arms of Natural History Society of Montreal : an owl perched upon the branch of a tree, and holding in its beak a small sprig. " Motto, " TANDEM FIT SURCULUS ARBOR." Rev. Within a beaded circle a garter inscribed, " PALMANIQUE MERUIT FERAT ;" inside of garter, " PRIZE MEDAL ;" outside of circle, " NATURAL HISTORY SOCIETY MONTREAL." Size 24.

36. Obv. Between two branches of palm, a shield, from the top of which issue diverging rays, a small maltese cross between colors, bearing in its first quarter, a Latin cross ; second, an open book ; third, an even balance ; fourth, a serpent entwining a wand. Within a circle, " DEO . FARENTE . HAND . PLURIBUS . IMPAR." Outside of the circle, " UNIVERSITÉ LAVAL QUEBEC." Rev. A wreath of laurel. " PRIX DE POÉSIE FRANÇAISE." At top between two palm branches a shield bearing an open book. Size 26.

The dies for this medal were executed by Mr. George H. Lovett, of New York.

37. Obv. View of Crystal Palace, Toronto; above " CRYSTAL PALACE ;" below, " 1858 TORONTO." Rev. Arms of Upper Canada. (Now Ontario.) Size 19.

38. Obv. A square altar, above which are two hands clasped, and holding a lighted torch. " WILLIAM DUMMER POWELL AND ANN MURRAY INTERMARRIED 3RD OCTOBER 1775." Rev. Within a circular wreath in eight lines, " TO | CELEBRATE | THE | FIFTIETH | ANNIVERSARY | UPPER CANADA | 3RD OCTOBER | 1825." Size 23.

Mr. Powell was for many years Chief Justice of the Province, and during a visit to England, in 1825, he caused dies to be prepared, and these medals were struck for circulation among his personal friends. They were in gold, silver, and copper, and the number struck was about 60 in all. We have never met with a copy, and are indebted to Mr. Groh of New York for a rubbing, from which we take the description.

39. Obv. Starting from bottom, and extending two-thirds up each side of Medal is a wreath of May flower; on top, " TEMPERANCE SOCIETY." Within wreath, " TOKEN OF MEMBERSHIP." Rev. Similar wreath to that on obverse; above " NOVA SCOTIA ;" within wreath in three lines " UNION IS STRENGTH ;" below which is a Maltese cross. Size 24.

40. Obv. Very large bust of George III. to right, laureated and wearing a mantle secured in front by a large bow of ribbon. Over the mantle is laid the collar of the order of St. George, with the Jewel attached. " GEORGIVS III DEI GRATIA BRITANIARUM REX. F : D :" Below the bust in small letters, " T. WYON JUN SC." Rev. Royal Arms of Great Britain. " 1814 " below. Size 48.

During the War of 1812, many of the Indians maintained their loyalty to the British crown, rendering valuable services, and at the conclusion of the war the government being desirous of marking its appreciation of these services, besides other presents and grants, caused this medal to be struck (in silver) and a copy was distributed among the chiefs and principal warriors of the tribes. It will be observed that the medal is very large, and weighs $4\frac{1}{4}$ ounces. The object of striking such a large medal was probably to please the well known desire exhibited by Indians for something showy and attractive. This medal is rare ; one or two specimens having been sold for $12. The medal has a loop for a ribbon to be attached.

" In 1813 the Americans formed a grand plan of operations against Montreal. Two armies were to co-operate in this enterprise, the one of 6,000 men under General Hampton, from Lake Champlain ; the other 8,000 strong under Major General Wilkinson, from Sackett's Harbour on Lake Ontario. Hampton found himself opposed at Chateauguay by a body of Canadians and Indians under DeSalaberry and McDonnell, who manœuvred their small force of 400 so judiciously that General Hampton thought it prudent to retire.

" Wilkinson's force entered the St. Lawrence, and two detachments of 1000 each were landed at Williamsburg to disperse the Canadians who harassed their passage. The Americans under Boyd were attacked by a force under Morrison, and on November 11, the battle of " Chryslers Farm " was fought.

At the close of the war the British Government distributed to the Canadian regiments which had taken part in those engagements, the ordinary Peninsular War Medal (silver), but having clasps inscribed " CHATEAUGUAY " and " CHRYSLERS FARM." There is also said to be a clasp for " DETROIT," but such has not come under our notice.

These medals, (indeed any English War Medals), are but rarely found in collections. The law prohibits any person from purchasing medals from a soldier or his friends under a penalty of fine or imprisonment, and the confiscation of the medal so purchased. This law renders it necessary that caution should be exercised (that is in British possessions) in purchasing these articles. The following is a description of the medal:

41. Obv. Head of Victoria to right; below " 1848." Rev. Victoria crowning the Duke of Wellington. " TO THE BRITISH ARMY 1793-1814." Size 24.

An engraved portrait of Colonel de Salaberry (published some years ago,) has attached to it the *fac simile* of a medal bearing the reverse described; but the obverse is a wreath of laurels, surrounding the word " CHATEAUGUAY." Whether such a medal was struck, we have not been able to obtain any reliable information, but we have been informed that it was " a special presentation medal to the Colonel."

42. Obv. In centre a cannon; above " FORT ERIE ;" below " JUNE 2ND 1866." Rev. In circle, above " PRESENTED BY THE ...... COUNTY OF WELLAND." Size 22.

This medal was struck in Montreal, and was intended to be presented to the members of the Welland Field Battery who had taken part in the engagement between the Canadian Volunteers and a body of Fenians during the Raid made in 1866.

[NOTE.—In addition to the medals described in this work, there are two or three University medals belonging to the Province of Ontario and to Nova Scotia, but having been disappointed in receiving information, we are compelled to omit them.]

NUMISMATIC & ANTIQUARIAN
SOCIETY OF MONTREAL.

———

In the month of December, 1862, several gentlemen of Montreal, desirous of cultivating the study of Numismatics,—and judging the formation of a properly organized association as the most efficacious means of attaining that end, assembled and formed " The Numismatic Society of Montreal."

The seal of this society was the obverse of the Canadian bronze cent, with an ·outer circle inscribed " SOCIÉTÉ NUMISMATIQUE DE MONTRÉAL. FONDÉE 1862." (See frontispece.)

On the formation of the Society, the attention of members was directed to Numismatics *in general.* It was not long, however, before several members very naturally directed their researches towards the Coins of Canada. The comparatively great variety,—the artistic excellence of numerous specimens, — and divers curious incidents bearing on these coins, furnished ample material for many interesting reflections and surmises.

Few persons, outside of the Society, appear to have been aware of many of these interesting facts,—indeed the existence of several of the coins which have been described, appears to have been altogether ignored by many. With a view, therefore, of bringing Canadian coins more generally under the notice of Numismatists and others, a Committee was appointed in 1863 to prepare a Catalogue of the coins. This work was commenced but never completed.

In January, 1866, the name of the Society was changed to that of the " Numismatic and Antiquarian Society of Montreal," and a new seal was adopted, viz.: a round shield quartered by a tomahawk and calumet, bearing an antique lamp, an ancient coin with head of

Minerva, a Canadian cent with head of Victoria, and a Beaver; the
shield encircled with a garter bearing the words, " NUMISMATICÆ ET
ARCHEOLOGICÆ MARIANOPOLITANÆ SOCIETATIS SIGILLUM." (See
Frontispiece.)

In addition to the study of Numismatic science, the members now
directed their attention to Antiquarian research, and the result of the
extended sphere of study has been to largely increase the membership, and the interest in the Society. Since the organization of the
Society, many very interesting and able papers have been read, which
it is hoped will be published at some future day.

The Society's cabinet has been enriched by several valuable dona-
tions of Coins and Medals, and the Library contains many works
upon Numismatic and Antiquarian subjects. The members are desirous of co-operating with similar Societies throughout the world,
and will be happy to open and maintain communications upon subjects of general interest. At present, the attention of the members is specially directed towards securing a complete collection of
Canada coins and medals, of which some very fine specimens are
already found in the cabinet.

This is the only Numismatic Society, (so far as we can learn),
existing in the Dominion, but we hope soon to hear of others being
formed.

www.ingramcontent.com/pod-product-compliance
Lightning Source LLC
Chambersburg PA
CBHW020313090426
42735CB00009B/1328